RADICAL

LOVE

IN AND OUT OF HIS CHURCH

ELIZABETH PRINGLE

Outskirts Press, Inc.
Denver, Colorado

Outskirts Press, Inc.
http://www.outskirtspress.com

ISBN: 978-1-4327-3267-7

Library of Congress Control Number: 2008940006

Outskirts Press and the "OP" logo are trademarks belonging to Outskirts Press, Inc.

PRINTED IN THE UNITED STATES OF AMERICA

...To follow Christ means to accept the *inner* essence of the cross, namely, the radical love expressed therein, and thus to imitate God himself...To follow Christ, then, means to enter into the self-surrender that is the real heart of love...

Pope Benedict XVI

A Letter to the Catholic Laity

Dear Brothers and Sisters:

What is it that God wants from us? If you're not sure, I'll tell you what I know. Relationship! Intimacy! Love! Truth! Happiness! You! That's what Jesus hungers for. He wants you! You're who he died for and it's you he lives for. To get there we have to become ordinary holy people. I want that. Don't you?

As I share some of my life-changing testimony I'll throw a few things your way that you may find totally shocking. That's OK, there's room for all of us. It's not about being right, after all, it's about shaking a stick at old thinking and checking out how it's working. I'm a joyful creature and life is humorous, so don't take it amiss if I seem to appear irreverent on occasion. No offense intended. The point is this. Are you open to taking another look at your faith, at what you really believe and where you are in your relationship with the Father who loves you and the Church he gave you to get you to him?

Come! Have some fun with my book and expand your vision, the vision we were given from Vatican II in the 1960's, promulgated by our dearly beloved Pope John Paul II and beautifully continued by Pope Benedict XVI in his heart of love for all. I am Catholic to my bone so let me pour some thought-provoking juice into the mix to get you talking and to open up the dialogue in your home and maybe, yes, just maybe, even in your Parish. My, my, my, wouldn't that be something! Sitting over a cup of coffee in the Parish Center, jawing over this book, agreeing to disagree yet finding enough to discuss, to wonder, if you really know all you think you need to know about God in your life. There is always more, so much more! It's an adventure. Enjoy the ride and enjoy the book!

Your sister in Christ, in love,

Elizabeth

Acknowledgements

For their love, support and encouragement with this book,
it is my pleasure to acknowledge:

Fr. Michael Scherrey, CC
Fr. Ed Wade, CC
Fr. Roy Ontiveros, O.Carm
Fr. Tom Alkire, O. Carm

Cora Cordoba, my long-time friend
Suzanne Young
Lupe Serenil
Barbara Jones
Coleen Ethridge
Georgia Anne Ethridge
Liz Silva

Most of all, my love and gratitude go to my heavenly Father
and Mother, Beloved Jesus and the Holy Spirit, the Angels and
Saints, without whom this book would never have been conceived
far less published.

TABLE OF CONTENTS

CHAPTER ONE
HERE SHE COMES, READY OR NOT!

"Oh, how I suffered, how I suffered with you," she would say, glazing over and disappearing into inner space. "The gutters ran with my blood: you can ask anybody."

How many times would I have to hear it? What was I supposed to do? I never knew what to do. I would try to arrange my little face into an acceptable format, eyes round with apprehension, holding my breath, yet somehow knowing that she didn't even see me. I think she was saying it for herself. What could I say, anyway? Sorry, Mummy, that I was born? Well, surely I was that, but I only once tried saying so. It brought on such a spate of grabbing and squeezing that I never tried it again. "Love" words spat out of her mouth. I pulled my head into my shoulders and ducked, as they flew past my ears, like bullets. Scary deal, this thing called love.

Of course, I get it now—the birth of a child is always dramatic—but mine, apparently, warranted an Oscar. It seems I was much too big for my laboring mother, and she spent the rest of our lives cutting me down to size to ensure that never happened again. Mummy became big, very big, and baby was to be small, very small, and that was how it was to be. I learnt my place early in life.

I was the third child to push my way out of her reluctant canal, and my emergence was the final stab through her already broken heart. For nine agonizing months, she had focused on "it's a boy, it's a boy", as though the saying of it would make it so. Obviously, she didn't get her way. She got me. Too bad. I was the death of her dream and the beginning of my nightmare, but the story doesn't start here, with my birth. It began, actually, with a death, the death of my brother, her first-born, who was gone long before I appeared and, yet, was the reason for my existence. It is astonishing how much significance we can take on before we're even here.

Her boy was gorgeous, truly. It's as though he were exceptional since his life was to be condensed. He was plump and juicy, full of mischief, with bursting rosy cheeks and great brown eyes sparkling with laughter and intelligence. I would fill with an unequal mixture of pride and jealousy when I saw the few pictures they had of him, my big brother. He was adored and knew it! Irresistible! It was easy to imagine him, running down the street with the cold Scottish air grabbing at his lungs, while he laughed and laughed with vim and vigor. He was the light of their lives, the joy of their being.

Then, a dreadful thing happened. Truly awful. At the beguiling, wonderful age of two and a half, he ran once too often. He chased his renegade toy out of the newspaper shop and right out into the middle of a busy Glasgow street. Wham, and it was over. His light went out and so did our mother's. The moment the bus hit was the moment she saw him under the screeching rubber. The driver never stood a chance, and neither did Jim. He was gone, his little life snuffed out, just like that, in a breath. She was seven months pregnant when she witnessed her precious child, her son, her wonder boy, under the wheels of a bus, still and gone. What, in the name of God, happened to her in that frozen moment in time? And what about the child in her womb, who wasn't a boy either? What about her? Fate was mapped out for that baby, too, in guilt and fear and grief, before she was even born. She arrived, two months after the event, to a mother who had become a virtual zombie in a lost world of darkness and mourning. Dear God! How terrible for both of them.

For the first year, my sister was abandoned to Aunt Sarah, who, fortunately, was sweetness and kindness itself, a truly gentle spirit who dearly loved her little namesake. Years later, on the sad day when we got news that Aunt Sarah had died, my sister was uncharacteristically undone. She was in her late teens, and she was crying. She never cried! I was shocked. "What's wrong? Why are you crying so hard?" I asked.

"My mother just died," she screamed at me. "That was my

mother." Ouch! That stung! So who was the woman in the other room, then, I wondered? I had no clue what my big sister meant.

Meanwhile, with the baby off her hands during the day while Father was working—oh, yes, there was a father, sort of—Mother would empty a trunk full of her boy's clothes, wash, iron, and replace them neatly, only to do it all again the next day. For an entire year, she did it. On one occasion, I asked her what stopped the craziness.

"Your father burnt the lot," she said. "He couldn't take it anymore. Said he had to, for both of us. So I took an iron poker to his head; I wanted to kill him. That stopped me; he stopped me."

He was strong as an ox, that man, a typical, stalky, broad-shouldered Scot, so it's no surprise that he caught her up short. It does say something about her state of mind, though, to say nothing of his! You must admit, this family is nothing if not colorful! After that, she made a stab at picking up her life, and her baby came home to stay. However, bitterness won out and rooted in her gut. She turned against God and her Catholic faith until both were as cold and dead as the stone on Jim's tomb. Her marriage followed suit.

One day, when I was about thirteen, she showed me her one solace. She kissed a tiny, ragged newspaper clipping that she folded and unfolded as she dug for the strength to share it. She told me, more or less, that the Magistrate stated that the run-over child was "healthy, well cared for and finely dressed, therefore there was 'no neglect'". Here was the proof that she was a good mother. It said so, didn't it? And I'm sure she was which only added to the tragedy. So, how could it happen? I can only think she was preoccupied. On that ominous day, when they had been shopping together, she had promised to buy sweets for the child, had forgotten and come home without them. She felt so badly about breaking her promise that she determined to go back out to get his sweets, despite the lateness of the hour. But what did she do? She bathed him, dressed him in his best, beautiful, satin sailor suit, and took him with her. Just to nip down to the corner shop? Was it serendipity? Was it just his time to go? Who knows. He certainly changed all of our lives by his brief appearance. She says she was afraid to leave him with Father, who admittedly fell asleep at the drop of a hat, for fear of the boy falling into the open fire. For only five minutes, or ten at most? It's a mystery, but there you have it. The boy never came home, and they eternally blamed each other for his death. They did stay married, their common ground being bondage to their loss. Hardly grounds for happiness, for anyone.

Mother was of Irish lineage, kept herself to herself, musical and feisty. My father, in total contrast, was a lowland Scot, raised in the Kirk with nothing but self running in his blood, yet outgoing and very likeable for all that. Prior to Jim's death, she had been ardent in her faith, my father not at all. She insisted they had to marry in the Church, so they did, not that he could care. True to form, he would do and say anything required of him to get the girl. Once done, he quickly reverted to his original distaste for her religion—until the death of his son, that is, when it escalated to real hatred of God and the Church. The more he wallowed in self-pity and fury at my mother's "negligence", the more he found family life to be untenable.

She was desperate to regain his favor and thought she could do so by producing another son. He turned her down flat on the grounds that she couldn't be trusted with a child. She begged, she pleaded, but he was adamant. As pressure grew, he withdrew. He had to get out; he just had to. In a crazed attempt to escape her nagging and, doubtless, to outrun blame and guilt, Mother found him searching the Classifieds for work in London. She panicked, and, as only she could, turned her fear into mockery, goading him into believing that he didn't have what it took to leave Scotland and head for England. Big mistake! She didn't know her man! Not only did he leave Scotland, he went one better and found employ with Crown Colonies and took off for West Africa instead.

There was no European family life in equatorial West Africa in those days, unlike Kenya or Rhodesia. It was not for nothing that it was called "The White Man's Grave". Disease was rampant, with little by way of medication to stand against Malaria, Black Water Fever, Yellow Fever and only God knows what all else. My father was no fool; in fact, he was extremely intelligent. You have to admire his strategy, but he didn't take into account the power of his strong-willed wife. My mother was a force! She went after him! She did! All the way to Africa in 1938, and she wasn't the size of tuppence. Five foot tall, though I'm not sure she was even that! Small women can be like terriers. When you're not looking, they'll get you in the ankle and never let go! What got into her to chase him down? In his absence, she had become obsessed with the idea that another son would win the day. Despite his reluctance and many protestations for her to stay home with her child, she abandoned my sister to Aunt Sarah once again and set off for the shores of Freetown, Sierra Leone. She was gutsy, if nothing else!

In childhood years, I was enraptured by her adventures and capitalized on her jaunts to foreign parts by indulging my imagination to the max. I would balance her many felt hats, one on top of each other as they were worn, unbelievably, to keep out the sun, but surely destined to bring on heat exhaustion instead! They were beige, apple green and white, though I think there was a fourth, and they leaned like the Tower of Pisa under my "bridal veil" of mosquito netting as I strutted toward my "jungle nuptials". Little did I know that I was setting a path for exotic adventures that would hold me enthralled for much of my life.

Talking of weddings, I suppose my priest story begins with the one who married my parents, or I wouldn't be here at all. It's fascinating how we have a part to play in each other's lives, whether we know it or not.

I don't recall ever hearing details about that veiled trip but her success was evident and went before her. She was, indeed, pregnant but not with the much hungered for boy. God help us all; she got me! When she was close to full term, Father returned to Scotland in anticipation of the birth of the son they believed was to be restored to them. I would go so far as to say that they were romancing reincarnation. They had staked their lives, their marriage, their future, their very happiness on this boy. And they got me, a bad omen, brought forth in rivers of blood, or so she said. There was no help for them. They never got over it, and my mother never tired of relating 'the moment' when she got the bad news. The exhausted and disappointed doctor announced, "Silk stockings again." My taste for beautiful things was already apparent! Joking aside, the final nail was that she could have no more children, and I had ruined her. Or, so she said.

Her failure to produce a son and heir sealed the fate of all of us. She hadn't completely lost her husband in that he always supported us financially but he could not wait to jump ship back to Africa. We were to live in a way that was not uncommon to Brits at that time. The men would be overseas in the Colonies, and the families remained in the UK until the children were old enough to be left or to join their parents. He stayed long enough to take care of the legal arrangements. I needed to be registered, and, for whatever reason that is beyond my comprehension, but could only be God, he also arranged a baptism.

Enter Fr. James Kearney, of St. Paul's Church, Shettleston, Glasgow, Scotland, who was ready to do the honors and baptize this thirteen-day-old infant, though why he should have is beyond me. All went well until he got to, "Elizabeth, I baptize you in the name of the Father, and of the Son, and of the Holy Spirit".

My mother piped up, "Elizabeth? You mean 'Janet!'"

The priest, taken aback, replied, 'Elizabeth' is the name on the Birth Certificate."

She persisted, "It can't be. There has to be a mistake. She was named Janet, after me."

I can only imagine the blank expression on the face of the priest as he shook his head, looking from one to the other for an explanation. Trust the Pringles to put on a show! She knew my father well enough by now, and it didn't take her long to connect the dots. He got her, didn't he? This was his way of taking revenge for her failure to produce a son. The cunning fox had named me Elizabeth without her knowledge. It was a name she hated, and well he knew it. He had named me after his Presbyterian mother for whom there was no love lost, the mother who had nothing but raw hatred for his Catholic bride and her Catholic offspring. It was his ultimate rejection of both child and mother: a cold legacy in a dark world, which was to get even darker. Then he left. A few weeks later, on September 3, 1939, a day never to be forgotten, Britain was at war against Nazi Germany. It had to be the end of the line for this heartbroken woman fresh from childbirth with an unwanted infant, a four-year-old child, a war on her hands, and now no man.

Nevertheless, what was the end of the line for her was the beginning of hope for me. See what God did. He has told us that when our mother and father put us down that he would pick us up (Ps 27:10). That's what he did, for me, with baptism. The sacraments are amazing! He picked me up that very day, true to his word and got me baptized, despite a God-hating father. He placed me in his family, his Church, the only one I was ever to know but not for many years. Thank God for Fr. Kearney, just doing his job. Bless him. That was the beginning of the miraculous in my life.

What else did God say? What others intend for evil, he will turn to good, if we're up for it, of course. I would have been ashamed to be named after the loathed grandmother, had I realized it. But I was always called Betty, Little Betty Pringle, that was me, running here, running there, always on the go. I knew no different until I left my village school and went to Buckhaven High School at the age of twelve. At roll call, they called out Elizabeth, and I didn't respond. Forty-five kids were stretching their necks to see what was going on when it became obvious that nobody was answering. Then the teacher asked who was from Lundin Links? Aha, that was little me, no problem. Did I not know my name, she asked? I was mortified and humiliated; from that day, for six years, they called me "Miss Lundin Links", the name of my village. I don't think they meant it cruelly, but it certainly compounded that I was "different". As if I didn't know! Rejection is a badge of shame, is it not? Yet, we don't even know when we're carrying it. We just feel "different". Buckhaven was a tough, mining area, and Lundin Links was of a gentler residential nature with golf, swimming, tennis, flannel dances and all that good stuff. To help things along, snobbish Mother sent me to elocution lessons, for heaven's sake, so I spoke like nobody that anybody had ever heard before. Wonderful! Instant alienation — just what I needed.

Elizabeth! In one fell swoop, my clever father managed to shame me, at the same time as he wanted to "claim" me, for "his side", and, simultaneously, managed to demolish his wife. Now, this is where God comes in, again. I believe he prompted the Holy

Spirit to move that hating father to name me Elizabeth because it is a holy name, a beautiful name. Where did Mary run when she was in fear for her life and that of her Son? To her cousin, Elizabeth, a safe place. I am humbled and grateful to have such a name. That's God for you.

In addition, the day of my baptism was August 6. That is the great feast of the Transfiguration of the Lord, when Jesus, on top of Mount Tabor, was transformed into a gleaming, brilliant whiteness. I believe that was God's prophetic promise to me. It was also when he proclaimed Jesus his Beloved Son and told the apostles to listen to him. I believe he claimed me as his daughter on that extraordinary day and put it in me to seek Jesus and listen to him, to his every word, and I do. (Luke 9: 28-36). That's what God did for this child.

My life began in the very heart of God's compassion and mercy. I lived a worldly life until I was in my forties; yet, looking back, God's hand was always upon me. As it began, so it continues, with ever more revelation. Fr. Sean Wenger, CC, says he celebrates his baptism more than he does his birthday. That struck me as odd, at first, but it makes perfect sense when you think about it. The way I see it now, we have three birthdays: born into the world, born into the Church at baptism, and born 'in spirit from above' into the Kingdom of God and an entirely new life. That makes Jesus a happy man! The three-fold birth is what it's really all about. That's our pathway to pure joy.

CHAPTER TWO
BACK FROM THE DEAD

It was World War II, May 1941. My sister was six, and I was twenty-two months' old. Glasgow was under bombardment. Our world famous shipyards were a magnet for Nazi bombing raids that never let up and rolled in at any time. My father was in Freetown, Sierra Leone, previously British West Africa, where there was a British military contingent. He wasn't "called up" to serve because he had curly feet, i.e. hammer toes that prevented him from marching, so he was off the hook and free to indulge the life he loved. Trust him to get away with it! Meanwhile, Mother was left alone to care for my sister and myself. Although she had family around during the bombing, it was, by necessity, every man for himself. My heart goes out to her when I think of her predicament. All the able-bodied men were off fighting Jerry, but I'm sure it didn't help one bit to know that many women were similarly up against it and barely coping.

She was terrified. Who wouldn't be? When the piercing air raid siren sounded and the lights from the ground fanned the sky trying to track enemy planes—hail, rain or snow, mid-day or midnight— that little mother had to grab her two kids, one by the hand and one in her arms, and join the throng descending the tenement stairs to the street. Once outside, the mad charge commenced to beat a path to the nearest underground shelter. Little as I was, I have a memory of my mother clutching me against her heaving chest as she begged a troubled face below ground to make room for us. She was sobbing with fear and gasping for breath in the cold night air, but the face was unrelenting, despite its obvious despair on her behalf.

"We're fu", lass," he said. "There's nae room, lass." "What about my babies?" she rasped. "What about my babies?" He shook his head with sadness and banged shut the metal cover. Off we went, run, run, run, as I bounced like a cork on her hip.

I do not doubt that my mother, rushed and petrified as she was, still took time to grab warm blankets to wrap around us; but no matter, I got sick anyway. I was so sick, in fact, that she sent a telegram to my father to get the next mail boat back to Scotland. I'm sure he was thrilled to traverse the Atlantic in the middle of a war when ships were going down every day; but he did, indeed, show up. The diagnosis was in. I had double pneumonia, which was as good as a death sentence prior to the advent of penicillin. It was a killer. Keeping in mind that my parents had already lost a child, to lose another was more than my mother could bear. All Herculean efforts to nurse me back to health failed. The fever refused to break, rendering the doctors impotent, and the dread day arrived when they had to admit that they could do no more.

"She's not going to make it," they said, "she'll be gone before the day is through. Better get the priest."

They did and he came. The Last Rites for the passing of the soul were administered, and slowly my labored breathing drew to a close, but not for long! I revved up again! I met Jesus on the other side! I did! There were no lights, no angels or bells, just darkness, as I recall, with Jesus standing far off with his arms open, palms outward. He looked like a shining star to this little girl, but he was definitely recognizable. I was on my way to him when he told me to stop.

"You must go back", he said. "My Father has work for you, and you will not see me again for a long, long, long, long time" (2 Timothy 2:11). I did as I was told and went back, bereft at the loss of him, but what he said was true. It was to be many a long year before I encountered Jesus again, but I lived!

That Sacrament is now called the Anointing of the Sick. It is for healing, not for dying, although, as you can see, it is useful for both! The change of title did not happen because the Vatican heard of me, although they should have, but because, apparently, it works! Another excellent thing that came out of it all is that I lost my flaming red hair for a less fiery brand, although I doubt I can say the same for my temperament. We can't have it all!

Therefore, yet again, another "ordinary" priest, just doing his job, exhausted in the midst of a war with the injured and dead all around him, hurried to the bedside of a dying child to save her soul. Little did he know he also saved her life. Guess he knows now. Beautiful, isn't it?

There is no such creature as an "ordinary" priest!

CHAPTER THREE
THE BAD SERVANT

I don't believe I encountered another Catholic priest until the early Sixties. I was married and living, wouldn't you know, in Freetown, Sierra Leone. I got the best of that charming city, on the edge of an azure blue sea, before its demise through a series of appalling civil wars. It's now a tragic wreck, hopefully trying to rebuild.

The day in question was Saturday lunchtime at our local watering hole, where the glad crowd would pack into the small bar at the Paramount Hotel to kick off the weekend. It was always a fun time. The men were done for the week, and we wives, all gussied up, would drive downtown to meet them for drinks and curry lunch and have a high old time of it. On this occasion, a priest was being feted with much ribaldry and jesting. He was Irish (What else?), no youngster and pleasantly grizzled. He had been upcountry in the bush for years and was on his way back home to Ireland, stopping only in Freetown to catch the plane out. My delightful friend, Tony Thompson, a Catholic himself, said, in dulcet tone and with mock shock, "Father! I saw you scoping the lady's legs!" They were mine, in the first era of the mini skirt, and I was more than a little embarrassed!

"Ah, boyo," said the Father with a twinkle, "just because you're on a diet doesn't mean you can't study the menu, now does it?" (I've heard this since but it was new at the time.)

His openness coupled with his broad smile brought the house down. I was relieved but are priests supposed to behave like that, I wondered?

I tell this little gem to demonstrate how God sets things up. The next priest I was to meet was so frightening to me that, had I not enjoyed my brief encounter with the first in Freetown, I doubt I would have had the courage to meet the second. However, I digress. Ah, yes, on with the story and back to Freetown. I became pregnant there. I'm told I was as pea green as the dresses I wore, usually my best color! At seven months, I went back to Scotland to have the baby, much to my husband's displeasure, but thank God that I did, or the baby and I would never have survived. He came to Scotland for the delivery from hell that left me with postpartum depression, a kidney infection, a botched and infected surgery, a baby with colic and dislocated hips, and months of snow and ice. He stayed for Christmas and the New Year, extended his home leave as much as possible but, inevitably, had to return to his work in Freetown. I remained in Scotland for another six months until our gorgeous little baby girl was taken out of the horrendous cage she was wearing to straighten out her hips. What a relief! It was a tough time with no friends or family around me. My kindly, hard-pressed mother-in-law did her very best, but I couldn't wait to get back to the balmy sunshine of the Africa that I loved.

Some months after my return home to Freetown, I took sick again. It was nothing I could finger, but I felt extremely lethargic and "spacey". With the benefit of hindsight, I see now that all sorts of things started to go wrong with my body after that episode. My African woman doctor was not the sharpest knife in the drawer at the best of times and seemed to have no solution to any of it except that I was "spoiled" and needed to go home and have a baby. That, by the way, would have killed me, the silly person! My first awareness that something was wrong was one summer evening at the Agip manager's home. We always had superb parties in Freetown, and this was no exception. The sweetly perfumed bougainvillea cascaded over the veranda onto the patio where we danced under the stars. It was a perfect tropical night, yet I felt cold, so cold that I wore my husband's jacket over my red chiffon gown. Hardly my normal fashion statement, yet none of us thought it strange. I remember wanting to leave early, which wasn't like me, either, being the heart and soul of the party kind of a person. I thought I was bored, which was absurd for such a delightful occasion, but it was what came to me. The following weekend we attended a buffet supper dance at the home of Tony and Terry Thompson, dear friends. I remember the slinky, blue and white floral-silk cocktail gown I was wearing, along with matching metallic-blue stiletto heeled shoes. It is said that we do that when something "fixes" in our brain; we remember what we were wearing. I felt ill. Nothing I could describe, just ill. I was sweating profusely even for equatorial Africa. I couldn't explain it; I just felt ill, everything was swimming before me, and I needed to get my wet clothes off and go to bed. Because we lived up the hill from our hosts, I decided to see myself home. My husband was enjoying himself; besides, he was never very nice to me, so I felt better off alone. I just couldn't handle his aloof coldness when I was feeling so staggeringly unwell.

I don't remember going to bed, but I do remember waking up with projectile vomiting of what I can only describe as green bile and I was burning up with fever. Thankfully, my husband was home. He looked tense as he hopped around on one foot, pulling on his pants and muttering something about a doctor. Fortunately, even in his panic, he had the clarity of mind to drive to the British army barracks nearby instead of trying to raise a doctor downtown. His quick thinking may have saved my life. The smart young Englishman took one look at me and was visibly shaken.

"How long has this been going on?" he asked.

"Just tonight," I replied.

"Rubbish, this has been going on for months," and he looked at my husband with fury, obviously wondering what planet he was on. After the examination, he sat on the edge of the bed, took my warm, dry hand in his and with tears in his eyes told me that he could do absolutely nothing for me, for four days. I was stunned. Four days seemed like an eternity. My eyes widened, questioningly, "Four days?"

"I think it's your kidneys. Can't be sure. You're a very sick girl. Have to grow a culture to see which antibiotic will respond to it. Hold on! Hold on for me!" And with a squeeze of the hand, he was gone. These four days were unspeakable, but I survived, and

15

the medicine worked over time. However, I was still unwell, and it was to be some time before I rallied into some kind of life. I lay prone on the sofa for many days. My poor little girl. All she ever knew was a sick mother. Doesn't make for happy times, does it?

Our prescribed time for home leave came around, which meant that we had to check in with the company doctor in London as a matter of course. We chose to do it before we went up to Scotland. After the usual niceties and uncomfortable shuffling of papers, he raised his head, stared at me and said, emphatically, "I haven't seen you. Do you understand me? Come back when you've seen a doctor where you're going, then I'll pass you."

Bother! That meant we had to come back through London on our way back to Freetown. I remonstrated with him.

"I have been ill," I said, "but I'm doing fine now." He just shook his head and said, kindly, "Go."

"Whoa," I thought, "what's wrong with him, I'm perfectly well now."

As usual, I did as I was told, and when we got to Edinburgh, I visited my husband's family doctor. He took one look at me, closed the clinic, put me in his car and drove me to the hospital. That was extraordinary! What on earth is going on, I wondered? He took me to a redheaded, rugger-playing, burly Scot named Dr. Murdoch. This was not a man with whom to argue! He admitted me right away and began running tests. Turned out I had Pylonephritis, a killer kidney disease. I was hospitalized for three weeks to see what they could do, either through a kidney removal or through medication. He was a great guy, tough and tender, the best kind. My husband was livid at the inconvenience of having me in hospital leaving him with our 15-month-old baby. Besides, he had a company junket to attend in Berlin, and he needed me home. He arrogantly informed the doctor that I was a malingerer, always sick and that this was a typical play for attention, that there was nothing wrong with me except that I was spoiled and drank too much cognac. Dr. Murdoch's eyes turned to steel and his jaw hardened. Oh boy! His retort was that they couldn't spare National Health beds in kidney wards for malingerers. Then he looked gently at me lying in the bed and said, "Tell you what, lassie. Drink a bottle. If you fall flat on your face, you've had too much. It's got nothing to do with anything", Then he spun on his heel and marched off. I grinned. Don't think he liked my husband! I had found an ally! Yippee!

We had home leave each year, so I was able to continue to check in with Dr. Murdoch regularly. Every time, he would give me a year's supply of Cycloserine and send me off with commands to bed rest when things got bad. It's not the first time I held a mini-cocktail party in the bedroom simply to enjoy the sheer absurdity of it! Chronic illness calls for creativity, and you gotta live, right? Can't afford to let it get you down, you know. Some years later, after my divorce and after a few years in Mauritius, I went to live in London. My medical care was transferred from Scotland, and I placed myself in the more than capable hands of the delightful Professor Brumfitt at the Royal Free Hospital in Hampstead, a charming part of town that I simply loved. He was the antithesis of my burly Scot. The professor was short, quick and dapper, with twinkling blue eyes that glowed with intelligence and the sheer joy of life. He took a shine to me and kept me going with a variety of antibiotics, but there was no denying the steady decline in energy and the number of infections piling up one behind the other, mostly e-coli. Where did I pick that up? Africa? Messed up delivery of my child? Who knows?

Life in London was hard, especially after the life to which I had been accustomed. Twelve years after wrestling with this disease, I could barely hold my life together and was counting my steps just to get to work. One more, I would say. No way, I would argue. Half a step, then? Agreed. I would sit on garbage cans, walls, anything that would hold me up to get my breath and gain a little strength. And still I was holding down a job. Amazing. Apparently, there was nothing wrong with my head! Nevertheless, I was winding down. Before my last appointments with the Professor, I was just too tired to sit up in the waiting room, so I lay down on the floor. It seemed like a good idea to me. I didn't see the pathos in it at all. It just seemed sensible! That should have been a sign, don't you think, that something just might have been going more than a little wrong? I smiled up at the professor when he arrived. He looked down at me with his usual greeting of, "How are you?" and received my usual, stock response of, "Fine, thank you", but from the floor! Why do we do that? The lab had grown a culture from a specimen a few days earlier, so, he had the results. I was helped to my feet, and we entered his office. He looked somber, troubled, and cut right to the chase.

"Dear lady," he said, "I'm afraid that there is nothing more to be done. You have the innards of a geriatric, and you have, at the outside, three months left to live. I advise you to get your affairs in order. If you continue to work, you're looking at about six weeks."

I asked the rhetorical question, "Will you pay my rent?"

Of course, I had to work! My daughter was too young to be left and, besides, there wasn't a soul who really cared for her but me. She was a beautiful child but we were very alone. I couldn't possibly die. His suggestion was out of the question, but what to do? I had to find another way. I thanked the professor for all he had done for me and left. Well, there it was. He didn't have to tell me how sick I was. I was fevered, but that was nothing new. I was only thirty-seven though. I knew he spoke the truth, and yet I didn't believe for one minute that I was going to die and leave my child. It just didn't compute, but what to do?

At the time, I was renting a room in the home of a Catholic woman, Maureen, and her invalid son, and, thankfully, my atheism didn't bother them or the lively priest (yes, another one, and Irish!) who visited for a bite from time to time. I'm sure I was being prayed for without my knowledge, which is so very Catholic. Thank God it works! It is fascinating how God uses anybody, since he loves everybody, in order to get our attention. A girl in the office made mention of a German chiropractor in Harley Street who had diagnosed her problem and healed her. I went. In his clipped, Germanic way he said, kindly enough, "I will not charge you. You are very close to death. There is nothing to be done."

"I know", I said, "I've heard it before."

I read an article about the Queen's having a Dr. Blackie who took care of her health with homoeopathic medicines. Don't ask me how I found that doctor, but I did.

"I would love to help you, but you're too far gone, and it costs

18

a great deal of money".

I thanked her for not charging me either. Someone knew of a Chinese acupuncturist.

"We can help certain infections by strengthening the area around, but there is nothing we can do for your condition. So sorry."

Thank you for not charging me. I was done, finished. I couldn't think of another single thing to do. It's a strange thing, but I've found that after we've tried everything we know to do, often that's when God steps in. And he did for me.

Back at the flat, I said, "I'm so desperate that if somebody said to lie down and let a goat pee on me, I would."

Maureen looked at me strangely, as that was so unlike me to come out with such a phrase, that it got her attention. She asked if I really meant what I said. Well, sure, I had a daughter I had to live for. For myself, I would have been happy to let go and pass into oblivion, but what about my daughter? How old was she? Just fourteen? Unthinkable. Fortunately, she was tucked away in her expensive boarding school and missed what was going on at this time, but I had to find a way to keep going until she was older. Maureen was thoughtful, then said, "I might know someone who could help but I can't promise."

"Who?" I asked. "Who might be able to help?"

"Wait and see," she said. "All I can do is ask." Thankfully, I didn't have long to wait.

She was speaking of her daughter-in-law, Sanjay, who agreed at least to meet me. She was a timid girl, a pretty little thing, but cowed and very softly spoken. I was somewhat uncomfortable, as I hadn't a clue how she thought she could help. It was agony trying to get through the initial generalities without screaming, "How can you help me? Can we please get to it?" It was quite a challenge. I was in something of a hurry, you can imagine. We were all smokers, so I offered around my cigarettes and lit up. I passed my gold Dunhill lighter from better days down the line. When it got to Sanjay, she took it, held it for a moment, and then thrust it across the room like a red-hot coal. She leapt to her feet, excused herself with a headache and darted for the door. We were stunned. What on earth caused that, we wondered? Maureen said, "She picked up on something."

"What do you mean?" I asked. I had no clue what she was on about. "Picked up on what?" I prompted again.

"I don't know, but I know Sanjay. Something's going on. Something really scared her."

Over a lighter, I wondered? How weird.

Later that day, we got to talking about it again, and Maureen's curiosity got the better of her. Apparently, Sanjay had "second sight", or some such, and Maureen was convinced that the lighter revealed something about me. Finally, she succumbed to calling Sanjay to see what she could learn and left the room to make the call. When she returned, she looked angry and guarded.

"What's the matter?" I asked.

"You haven't been honest with me", Maureen flashed back.

"What do you mean," I asked. "Honest about what?" "Sanjay says you have been into some very dark stuff, and she wants nothing to do with you."

"Dark stuff? What dark stuff?"

"You know", she retorted, "don't lie to me. The occult. You've been into the occult."

"What's the occult?" I asked.

I truly knew nothing of such things. Nothing. Finally, she believed me. She called Sanjay again to beseech her to listen to me. Maureen knew better than anybody how sick I was and feared I could die at any time. She'd seen me crawl upstairs on my hands and knees more times than not.

Sanjay returned. When she arrived, she told us that she had "seen" something when she held the lighter, not because it was a lighter, but simply because it was in my possession. She said that she had seen a circle of black men doing some chicken ritual around a fire and that they were very, very powerful.

"Sounds like juju," I said.

"What is that?" she asked.

I explained, according to the little I knew, that juju was rampant in West Africa. People paid the witchdoctors to cast spells, and they really believed in it. What's more, it seemed to work, but it had nothing to do with the Whites, I said, because you had to believe, and we didn't. What absurd ignorance, but what can you do? She continued to question me until she was satisfied that I was as ignorant as I claimed. She agreed that I was very close to dying and only because of that would she "help" me. She needed more information. Her reluctance was palpable.

She asked if I had in my possession anything else from my days in Africa. I gave her my engagement ring. What she had to say, as she held the ring and stared off into the distance, was totally astounding.

"Who is the woman I see wearing a polka dotted turquoise robe and lying on a dark red sofa?"

"That's me," I said, shaken, "when I was a young mother, in Freetown. I was very sick, so sick that I would lie there all day looking at a book on the other side of the room and too lethargic even to ask a servant to bring it. You saw me, all these years ago. I was about twenty four or five."

She said nothing. Then, suddenly, she blurted out,"That wicked old man!"

In that instant, inexplicably, I knew exactly what had happened to me and at whose hands. My father had told us never to hire an old servant. They had too much in them from the old days, he said. One day an old cook came to the kitchen door looking for work. He had excellent references, although they were not particularly recent. He seemed pleasant enough, and I felt sorry for him, still trying to eke out a living at his age. So we took him on. I was often alone, as my husband used to have to go on trek with his work, but I wasn't troubled because I had the servants and my baby and the Thompson's who lived down the hill. I was all right.

Or, so I thought, until that dreadful day during the rains, that ceaseless, torrential, equatorial rain, when my life changed forever. The old cook turned up for work, eyes scarlet and glazed, and he was drunk on palm wine. That's strong, raw hooch that can make a man crazy. I was most uneasy and kept my eye on him while I played with the baby. He started ironing my husband's shirts, muttering all the while and digging the point of the iron into the shoulder seams, as though trying to rip them apart. I became more and more nervous and decided to send him home for the day, especially when I saw how fearful the Nanny was becoming. She took the baby from my arms as I approached the old man to tell him to leave.

"I no go", he said.

I was shocked. I told him again with the same result. I demanded the key to the back door. He wouldn't return it, and he wouldn't leave.

"You woman, you no go tell me nutting," he screeched. "Only de masta, only he say me go."

He let loose a stream of obscenities particularly aimed at white women and every disgusting thing he would like to see done to them, and not least to me. It wasn't pretty. No kidding, I was getting really scared. I held my breath and removed myself to the living room, hoping that he would calm down and just go, but no such luck. He followed me, continuing his graphic rhetoric. I was trying to think. I was afraid for the baby. I was afraid to go to the phone. Nanny was saying repeatedly, "You no go touch my baby, you no go touch my baby", which wasn't exactly reassuring but certainly was a shared sentiment. It confirmed that she knew something was up. I signaled to her to take the infant into the nursery. I thought they would be safer out of sight and away from me.

I decided to try diffusing the situation with "normal" behavior first, so I went into the pantry to choose things for dinner. I stood in the corner clinging to the shelves, desperately trying to think, when I felt a chill. He was too quiet. I spun around, and there he was, not three feet from me clutching an enormous copper pot above his head and poised to bring it down on mine. I stared him down and spat out, "Do it. Just do it! Give me the satisfaction and do it!" Don't ask me where that came from! He hesitated only long enough for me to dart past him to the phone. Of course, as luck would have it, with the rain, it was working only intermittently. I charged outside, instantly soaked to the skin, sliding up and down the drenched, muddy hill trying to raise a neighbor, a garden boy, anybody, but I couldn't find a living soul. Then panic! What about the baby when I was gone? Oh, no. Oh my God, somebody help us. I clambered back up the slippery slope and fell through the veranda door screaming her name, dripping water everywhere, and heard to my total relief, "We're here, Madame, we're here, baby good."

Thank God, thank God. The phone now worked long enough for me to get an urgent message through to my friends at the Paramount Hotel. Without hesitation or discussion, Ken and Pat were on their way, doubtless with tires screeching round the hairpin bends of the spur to come to my rescue. I could have sworn time stopped until Ken barged threw the door.

"Where is he?" he asked.

"In the kitchen, very drunk, full of hatred."

"Where's the baby?"

"With Nanny, in the nursery. They're alright."

He strode into the kitchen, closed the door, hit the old boy one time, took the key and threw him out the back door. Pat and I looked at each other with horror. We knew what Ken had done, we heard it, and it was not a good move. In fact, it couldn't have been more stupid. He was ex-army and old school but I had never seen this side of him. He was a perfect gentleman to all, normally. This obviously got him on the wrong side. My blood ran cold.

The cook ran to the front of the house and mounted the veranda, old as he was, wildly gesticulating his rage and hatred outside the window and shaking his fist, "No young missy go fire me. No young missy go fire me."

I filled with icy apprehension. The Baileys were greatly disturbed that I was on my own and wanted me to return to their hotel with them. For some absurd reason, I thought it would be better to keep a semblance of normality and stay in the house to avoid further upheaval, especially for the little one's sake. It felt wrong, somehow, to demonstrate any kind of fear. Idiot!

Now, I would have had the sense to leave but then? Well, I just wasn't mature enough or experienced enough to read the situation. Over the coming days, I could sense prowlers around the compound, but I convinced myself that they were just trying to scare me and would do me no harm. Not smart! In addition, the fact that they were succeeding didn't seem to enter into the equation! My nerves were raw. Although I believed I was safe with the night watchman and the other servants coming and going, these were restless nights until my husband came home. Of course, he knew nothing of any of it since there was no way to contact him up country. Besides, the damage was already done. We got another cook, and life went on until the memory of that day sank into oblivion. I loved Africa. I loved my life there and my many friends much too much to let something like that get in the way. Nevertheless, he got me—he got me big time, as they say—and without my even knowing it. What Sanjay saw in my ring was the result of his handiwork. He got me with juju, the mother and father of all witchcraft.

She nodded gently as I brought her up to date and finished my story. She knew. I didn't know what she knew, but I knew that she knew.

"I will try to help you. I know a priest, a Catholic priest, who might help you. He doesn't take everyone who comes along. I can only ask him, then it's up to him. I'm going out on a limb, for I am not supposed to do this, but I believe you will die if I don't. I'll see what I can do, but I tell you this. If he decides to take you on, you better do everything he tells you to do. Will you do it?"

"I will," I said, "You have my word."

Moreover, I meant it, and I kept it. I am so grateful to Sanjay and that family for allowing God to use them in that way. They saved my life. She looked into my eyes, nodded and took her leave. I had very mixed feelings; real hope sparked in me and so did real fear! A Catholic priest? What did that mean? Then again, I did say that I would try even a goat, didn't I? So how could I turn down a priest? If he agreed to see me, I just needed to see it through. After all, he was my last resort and the sands were running out. I hadn't long to wait.

CHAPTER FOUR
THE EXORCISM

His name was Fr. Anselm. He was a Discalced Carmelite, which meant that he trotted around in a long brown robe and sandals, although he looked more like a garden gnome to me than any idea of a priest. He was as wizened as a walnut, with jowls that shook in the breeze; he stood about up to my waist, and he was positively daunting! As I arrived at the monastery, I had a sense that he was waiting for me. He was basking in the sun, arms folded, eyes shut, with his backside propped against the wall. Somehow, I just knew that this gnarled old man was my priest. Trust me, I thought, to get one like that! I approached him.

"Father Anselm?"

His eyes popped open, bright as can be as he scanned my soul in a nanosecond, or so it seemed.

"I'm not a white witchdoctor you know," he shot back at me in an educated, clipped tone. "I don't go around reversing other people's folly."

I was shocked and, to my amazement, heard myself snap back, "I didn't expect that you were, and I'm appalled that you would even think that I would think such a thing!"

I cringed at my rude response and thought that I'd blown it, right off the bat.

"You'll do," he said, turning away as he shuffled towards the monastery. I stood stock still, trying to make him out and wondering if I wanted to go through with it. "Well, come along, child," he said, with a quick turn of the head, "We haven't all day."

I moved myself, blurting out as I went, "I have no faith in your

God," thinking I'd better come clean right away. It seemed air shattering to me; but without missing a beat, he said, "Oh, hush, child, I've enough faith for both of us." I followed him indoors. Now that really was shattering! There I was, one minute enjoying the warmth of the sun on my back and the brightness of a lovely summer's day and the next I was plunged into blinding darkness. I froze for a moment, blinking a couple of times to adjust my eyes. The place felt dank and ominous. I tried to shrug it off, reminding myself that it was only because the building was ancient—eleventh century I believe—with very thick walls and flagstone floors that added to the very real chill in the air. That's all it was, I was sure. Nevertheless, it gave me the creeps! From the monastery entrance, we went into the church. He genuflected and shoved on my arm to do likewise, both of us clutching the back pew, for different reasons, so as not to fall flat on our faces! Despite my debilitating sickness, I still decked myself out. Groveling around on the ground, indulging someone else's ritual was embarrassing in the extreme, but he had a way with him, did Fr. Anselm. He was quite a character, definitely one of God's peculiar people.

I had a little time to glance around and get my bearings while he prayed for a moment. It was dismal and strange, this church. It seemed huge. At the back, where we were, the old arched door was wide open, the sun streamed in, and there were tourists milling around all over the place. Down yonder, at the altar, in the gloaming of the bowels of the church, there was a service going on with a priest gesticulating before a handful of people, still as statues. In between, a sprinkling of others were looking around or just sitting there taking no apparent interest in anything. The entire scene gave me the shivers. It was so dim and gloomy that it bordered on the sinister; at least it did to this outsider. I was hard pushed to understand how anyone could embrace such an inhospitable and isolating religion, so joyless and dark. Perhaps that was the point, a place for miserable people to feel they were not alone amongst others of the same persuasion. Not for me, thank you. I hadn't given up on life just yet. I was still breathing, and that womb tomb was not for me. No sirree.

I was jarred back to my reality as Father tapped my arm and

pointed to a number of metal boxes on the back wall, inside the church mind you. They had coin slots and contained tracts and prayers. He made clear the ones he wanted me to buy: there, clink, clink, and there, clink clink. In a church! I found it all oddly discomfiting. Then he steered me to the shop on the opposite side of the corridor to buy a rosary. Thus armed, I was apparently ready to meet God. He told me to read everything he had given me, to say the rosary the best I could and to call him in a week. Then he was gone.

I endured the boredom of going through all the prayers and readings, but it wasn't particularly arduous, probably because I was reading and not praying. Maureen, my landlady of sorts, saw me hassling with the rosary and said, laughingly, "We don't pray them, Liz; we hang them on the bed." What a strange new world this was. I went through the prayers anyway, tedious though they were, just because I had promised that I would. One week later, I was back at the monastery. I was escorted to a simple room with a highly polished table, a couple of chairs and a leather armchair. Almost immediately, Fr. Anselm entered the room. With a nod, he lowered his old bones gingerly into the chair opposite me, settled down with a couple of sighs and appeared to go to sleep! Well, thanks very much! At first, I decided he was praying, but it went on a bit too long for my taste, so I started clearing my throat just to remind him that he was not alone. It had some effect. He started puffing, blowing, and muttering unintelligibly as though he was gearing up to something important. Not at all. That was it. That was all I got, huff and puff.

"Fr. Anselm, I can't hear you," I said. More muttering. "I can't hear you, Fr. Anselm, please could you speak up?"

He continued with his sound effects. I was stung and close to tears at being so ignored. How bad mannered, I thought, but then he was, wasn't he? He had to know that I was scared out of my wits with all that was going on with me without having to put up with weird religious goings on, too. No matter to him, it seemed. I felt like a piece of nothing. Suddenly, his eyes opened as he maneuvered himself out of his chair and standing up, said, "Same time next week, my dear?" and he was gone.

"My dear" sounds OK, but it doesn't always feel like it is. It can be friendly, but yet...it can also feel somewhat patronizing. Priests can be good at that. I don't think they know their own power either to lift up or to put down. No matter, the good book says not to do what they do but to do what they say. That was my job, so I got on with it. I did my reading, reading, reading, and maybe a little praying sneaked in by accident. The next meeting with Fr. Anselm was much like the first, but I started picking up words like "Adam and Eve", "the serpent", "the garden" and I realized that he was probably quoting the Bible. I was becoming more and more agitated with his treatment of me and unwittingly was turning more to God, crying out for help. The next time, I was polite but assertive. I started talking as he entered the room. I told him how hurt I was and mentioned, that when I was chatting with God...

"Stop," he said, sharply. "What did you say?" I held my breath. "Chatting with God, are you? Chatting with God, child?" he repeated, spitting out every word. "Where are the prayers I gave you? Do you have them?" Oh, Lord, I was dying a million deaths. What had I done?

"Yes, Father," I whispered, stunned at his reaction, "they're in my purse."

"Let me have them, child, all of them." I was mortified. I handed them over, feeling worthless at my audacity as to chat with God. I didn't know not to. He took all the prayers, Saint this and Saint that, tore them in pieces and threw them into the wastepaper basket. When he was done, he made his announcement, loud and clear, "Anyone who can chat to God has no need of anyone else's prayers."

It took me a moment to catch on. It was OK! He wasn't going to eat me alive after all. I was elated, infuriated, amused and puffed up all at the same time. He was something else, my little old priest.

After that, we talked. He was intrigued that I had no problem understanding the Trinity, which, according to him is the great mystery, yet I had a big problem as to why the Roman Catholic Church was THE Church, but he didn't labor it. All he needed to have told me was that it was the only church for sixteen hundred years. That would have made sense to me. No matter, all things in due course. Our meetings took place over a few weeks. Finally, he told me that he was certain that I needed exorcism (Matthew 12:28). Boy, that scared the heck out of me. Scary word! He explained that I had come under demonic influences, which needed to be driven out by the power of God. He explained, also, that you get only one, it being unnecessary to do more and he would perform it when the time came. Of course, I wanted it immediately, whatever it was. I wanted these influences gone, like now! I was still working, despite being so exhausted, but something more was going on than the sickness. I was restless and anxious, as though my nerves were flowering through my skin. I was having a monumental struggle trying to keep my emotions under control. I was normally fairly easy going, but not of late. I was becoming more and more agitated, hysterical and angry. Then one awful day, I really knew he had to help me.

It was in the office. I had become quite fond of an Irish Catholic girl who worked there. She was lively with long hair in a ponytail and a swanlike neck. One day she approached my desk, as usual, but this time all I heard and saw was a clucking, mocking chicken. It was all I could do not to put my hands around that long skinny neck and wring it until she was dead. Talk about panic! I rang the monastery and demanded that Fr. Anselm be there immediately for the time was now! Just by the way I spoke, they got it. I grabbed my purse, charged down the corridor, gasping for breath as anxiety gripped my throat and lungs and fell out into the street to hail a taxi to get myself over there. I could feel my eyes bugging out of my head with terror. Or was it horror? Or was it both? What on earth was happening to me?

I was shown into a room with only a huge floor crucifix for company, a podium, a table and a chair and was told that Father would be along shortly. I smoked and paced and paced and smoked. There was an ashtray available. In he came. I told him what had happened. He looked prayerful and thoughtful. That was the wrong response. There was no more time. I caught him by the neck, with both hands, lifted him clean off the floor against the wall and demanded my exorcism. This convinced him that it was,

29

indeed, the time! I let him go. He dropped, screwed up his nose, emptied the ashtray out of the window and left the room, saying, "I'll be right back."

"Ok, ok, but be quick. I'm going crazy," I replied with a nasty voice and a nasty look because I was becoming a very nasty person. I felt I was about to climb the walls or leap out of my skin or rip it off. I strode up and down, back and forth, to and fro, trying not to pull out my hair. My nerves were ripping through my skin. I'd no idea what was going on with me, but I know now. Fr. Anselm's tactics, which were never discussed, then or since, were to drive the demons crazy by ignoring them. They wanted to be the centre of attention. By ignoring me, he was attacking my pride. I hadn't told him that one of the worst punishments he could have inflicted on me was to give me the cold shoulder and ignore me. I'd had years of that in my marriage and I was still raw. Because of the "trigger," the spirits came to the surface and started kicking up (Revelation 12:7-9). That's when he was ready to deal with them. Dear God, I wanted these creatures gone! How I wanted the sickness gone! I had to live. I had to keep courage for this, whatever it was, as it was my only hope.

Back he came, staggering under a pile of ancient books, as could be seen by the condition of their discolored, cracked spines. He nodded to me to sit down at the table facing the crucifix and dumped the books alongside me. I don't recall bell or candle, but there sure were books. He joined me at the table and started thumbing through them, muttering away as usual. I believe he was praying, but who knew? I was relatively patient because I knew that what I had been waiting for was about to happen. The exorcism, whatever it was, would set me free. Oh, my God. Unbelievable! I realized it was about to happen. What I'd waited for and worked towards was here. I was shivering with cold. Don't know if it was the room or me. When the priest was satisfied, he got up and took his chosen books to the podium along with a Bible. I thought he was finally going to teach me something, but no, not at all! True to form, he went to muttering! Then I realized it was Latin. It was one of my better subjects at school, so it wasn't hard to recognize once I could hear it. Perhaps that's what he had been up to all along.

I sat there, as though in a trance, but not really. Just still, very still, with my forearms laid flat on the table in front of me. I was sufficiently compos mentis to be able to observe myself, and nothing was happening except the bizarre stillness. Then I heard an American voice, like a New York wise guy, whether in my head or around my head I do not know, and it never let up.

"So, what d'you want, huh? An Academy Award, huh? You think he doesn't get it, huh? He gets it, dummy, he gets it. Give it up. Give it up. You want an Academy Award...?" On and on it went, very clear, very male. I'd no idea at that time that I would end up in the USA where all things dark and light would be made clear to me. It was the last place the devil wanted me to be, so he tried to sicken me to it. At the same time, I was aware of the priest's voice droning on in the background. I didn't feel there was anything I was supposed to do except to just be there and sit it out.

Suddenly, both voices were silent. Father had stopped. He shook his head in recognition of something and, with jowls jiggling, he scampered from behind the podium to the table where I sat. He all but buried his head in the books, old back crouched over, not this book, not that one, not this one, then he blurted out, "We have the wrong spell, my dear, we have the wrong spell," but he wasn't troubled.

Quite the contrary, he seemed exhilarated. He was on a quest, and he could taste blood! Still I was silent, watching, listening, and somewhat spaced out. How does he know, I wondered. With all these books how could he begin to fight his way through them to know which spell was cast? It was troubling and frightening. My life depended on this ancient of days getting his act together!

And he did.

"There it is," he exclaimed, with delight. "I knew it! I knew we were on the wrong track! There it is! The spell was slow death. Yes, that's what it is. They wanted you to live a long slow death, my dear."

This time the "my dear" sounded lovely, encouraging and affectionate as though I were a real person.

"Now, we can get to work," he said.

Back to the podium he went, spry as could be, regenerated and muttering in Latin once more. Time went by, I really couldn't say how much, but from start to finish, it seemed about five hours. Once he found the spell he was seeking, I became aware of change, but it was all very subtle. My fingers began to move extraordinarily slowly in some sort of rhythm. Liquid oozed from my eyes and nose. I had the presence of mind to check it out: it was clear like water and non-viscose. I felt nerves haphazardly jump and twitch in my face. The strangest thing of all, and the hardest to tolerate, was the other thing that was happening to my face.

Have you seen children's books, sometimes made of cloth, where all the pages are slit into three parts so you can make many different pictures, or faces, by flipping the sections in different directions? My face was doing that! At the same time, each part was sliding sideways, so I never had a complete face. My forehead slid to the left as my eyes slid to the right as my cheeks slid to the left and so on. What with that and the incessant "American" wise guy that wouldn't shut up while Father was praying, I was irritated to the extreme but still immobile. My body remained stark still, never moving a muscle, and not a sound passed my lips throughout the entire process, just face and fingers. I just sat there, as though mesmerized. Finally, things settled down, and it was over. I felt out of time and space, kind of dazed, but aware enough to drive home. Or so I thought.

I don't recall anything being said apart from a quiet, "thank you" from me. I gathered up my purse to leave as Fr. Anselm held a ring to my lips and said, "Kiss it."

When I did, my forearms burst into flames. I kid you not, from elbows to the tips of my fingers I was burning in invisible fire (Matthew 25:41). I screamed. He just stood there and stared at me as though rooted to the floor.

"Don't just stand there," I yelled, "I'm on fire, I'm on fire! Do something! Help me!"

At that, he came out of his apparent stupor and scampered out the door. I heard his uneven gait, in his haste, thumping along the flag stoned floor. Dropping my purse, I tried to scrape off the flames with my hands, screaming all the while, but it was useless. On his return, with deep concern and carrying what looked like a piece of brown string, he held up a tract which I recognized and asked if I'd read it. I read everything he gave me, so I knew I had, but I was unable to speak or nod my head.

"Do you agree everything that is in it?" he asked.

I had no idea what was in it, but since he had given it to me, the answer was "yes", but still I could not speak or move my head. I looked at him frantically, still shaking off flames, willing him to hear my unspoken yes. He literally jumped up off the ground. He really was tiny, and I was in heels, yet he grabbed onto the back of my head with both hands and pulled it forward in a nod, then he threw the brown string around my neck. Instantly, the fire went out. Instantly! Total peace! The flames were gone. I stared at my arms that only seconds before were in torturous fire, turning them to and fro, as though to find some sign of what I'd just suffered. There was nothing, absolutely nothing, no trace at all.

"It's a trick," I said, appalled, looking at him. "It was a trick."

Immediately, the flames went to my feet, invisibly burning from knees to toes just as they had on my arms. "It's not a trick," I screamed, jumping up and down and kicking to get them off me. "It's not a trick," I yelled, hysterically.

And it stopped, just like that, with the snap of a finger. The fire went out, and the flames were gone. It was over. I looked at Fr. Anselm, then at my arms and feet, quite incredulous at what had just taken place.

"What happened?" I asked him. "What was that? I burst into flames, you know?"

"Yes, child, you did. I have seen many things but never that."

He was thoughtful, but calm, which helped me to believe that everything was all right and under control. "You can thank the Blessed Virgin of Carmel for your deliverance." How so, I wondered. Was it not the brown string thing that immediately quenched the fire? It was, I thought, but what was that string? As always with the things of God, there is mystery within the mystery. Let me tell you the story.

It is said that somewhere around the twelfth century there was a certain landed gentleman named Simon Stock, an Englishman from Kent, who had returned to his homeland from the Crusades in the Holy Land. He headed up the remnant of a religious order, the Order of Carmel that took its name from Mount Carmel, in Israel, where prophets had hung out in caves over many years, drawn there by the spirit of the great prophet Elijah. They also had a deep and sincere devotion to the Virgin Mary. Elijah was the one who brought down fire from heaven to conquer 450 satanic priests of Baal at one fell swoop (1 Kings 18:20-40). After that event, Elijah heard the sound of rain (1 Kings 18: 41-46). After many years of drought, a cloud the size of a man's hand, thought to be the Blessed Virgin Mary, appeared on the horizon and brought rain as a type of the Holy Spirit. Therefore, the Carmelites operated under the spirit of Mary and the Zeal and power of Elijah. While in deep prayer and crying out for guidance, Simon received a visitation from Our Lady of Mount Carmel. She was carrying a brown scapular, which is a covering like an apron. It is a long strip of cloth with a hole in the middle for the head to pass through. Mary said that the Carmelites were to wear this garment as their covering of protection and that she would save from hellfire anyone who wore it in good faith. Over the years, a third order of lay people developed, who wanted to embrace Carmelite spirituality; they wore a type of scapular representing Our Lady's protection and their allegiance to her service. It consisted of two small pieces of brown fabric joined by two strings that passed over the head. The tract that Fr. Anselm held up in front of me was the invitation to join the Confraternity of the Brown Scapular. My "yes" sealed it; in that moment, Our Lady of Mount Carmel, Mother of God, true to her promise, delivered me. The Blessed Virgin Mary visited me that terrible day and pulled me out of hellfire, for that was surely where this heathen was going. The Brown Scapular thrown over my head put to flight the demonic forces that were manifesting their rage as they saw me slip out of their deathly grip.

You want to know what happened after the Exorcism. The sickness was completely gone, completely. I went to see Professor Brumfitt who walked right past me in the waiting room at the hospital. He gave a cursory nod when I greeted him. Clearly, he did not recognize me. Apparently, my entire visage had changed.

When I assured him who I was, he called for the students and my file. He gave a rundown of the previous years of treatment when he had pronounced me good as dead, then he asked what I had done. Fr. Anselm had told me to keep it to myself, so I just said, "I can't really say."

After examination, he said, "This was some kind of faith healing, was it not?" I nodded. He said, "Say no more. This was quite beyond man to do. Good luck to you. You are well."

However, I had three more exorcisms, not because of the sickness, but because of spiritual manifestation and attacks of various kinds. Fr. Anselm wanted me to join the Church. Oh, no, I thought, I can't do that. I just can't do it. He was amazed.

"Why do I need to?" I asked.

"For protection, child."

"I can't take it on as an insurance policy," I said with sadness. "It's so horrible a place. When did you last look, Fr. Anselm?" I pleaded. "When did you last really look in there, really look at the people, at their faces? I'm a free spirit, and you want to lock me up in there, in darkness and death? Please don't make me do that, please," I begged, close to tears.

"Very well, child, but you're going to have to do it the hard way."

I remember looking at him, quizzically, wonderingly, as though there were any other way to live, for I knew no other way and said as much.

"Then, go your way and go with God, but be sure to say these four prayers every day of your life", he said, which I did. They were the Creed, the Our Father, the Glory Be and the Hail Mary and, unbelievably, that simple obedience saved my life—yet again.

I gave my Exorcist two bottles of vintage wine for his trouble, thinking I was doing just fine, and took my leave. Did it occur to me that he had put his life on the line for me? Not at all, of course not. I was grateful, surely, but it was God who did it, wasn't it? The priest was doing his job, wasn't he? He didn't need to do it, did he? It was his choice after all. How many of us think like that? What deplorable ignorance! God forgive me. Only the Lord, and maybe Father Anselm's brothers, maybe, knew what that precious priest had been through in order to be able to perform these great and mighty works of God to set people free.

This I do know, no one seeking appreciation, honor and respect had better choose the priesthood! You will be persecuted. That's a promise!

CHAPTER FIVE
A BRAND NEW LIFE

In 1980, some time after regaining my health, I was ready to resume my travels. It hit me one Saturday, on a summer's day in London with the wind and rain banging against the window that it was definitely time to leave! I sat, disgusted and cross-legged, in the middle of the lounge floor and studied a map of the world. Where could I go? Supertramp was on the radio, pounding out "Breakfast in America," and that was that. I thought of all those folks, in shorts and T-shirts, thronging to Denny's in blazing sunshine, and the decision was made. America, here I come! I packed up and headed straight to Houston, Texas, intending to stay for maybe a couple of years. I think I had Australia in the back of my mind. I had tried to get there once before, via Mauritius, having spent many years on that lovely island, but at that time I needed to be in the UK with my daughter, so it fell through. Why not go the other way? I just used to wander the globe wherever "fate" took me and the signs were pointing to the USA.

It was in my second year in Houston that I fell ill. I had a German friend, Crista, a nurse, who worked for an excellent doctor who referred me to the famous Texas Medical Centre for a battery of tests. While they were processing, I struggled on, but I knew I was rapidly weakening. Then I got the news.

It was a Sunday, humid, balmy, hot, dazzling sunlight, just the way I liked it. Even better, I was simply nipping round the corner to lunch with a Brit friend, Ann, and our mutual friend Crista. It was pushing it a bit because I felt lousy, but I so much wanted to enjoy my friends that it was worth it to me. When I got there, Ann was in the kitchen putting the final touches to our meal. She was a great cook, and I leave much to be desired in that area, so I was looking forward to the treat. These things truly keep sick people going. I helped myself to a gin tonic, ice and lemon, popped a cigarette in its holder, lit up, and settled on the floor with my head propped on the crossbar of the bar stool. I was ready to party, but felt too exhausted to sit up to do it! That was typical of me, at the time, doing the absurd to avoid the obvious.

I was happy to be there and happy to hear Crista's lilting, "Hi, sweetie," as she greeted me, with her broad smile. I glanced up, grinning, but immediately sensed that something was wrong.

"What's up?" I asked, quizzically.

She darkened a little, frowned at my smoking, which was water off a duck's back, and said, quietly, "I'm so sorry, honey." She called everyone honey, more American than the Americans!

"What is it?" I asked again, but seriously this time. Ann stopped stirring, spoon poised in the air, as we both looked at Crista. Whatever could it be?

Her eyes travelled from one to the other of us and then she said to me, "I've made an appointment for you to see the doc. tomorrow. We have the results of your tests. You're in real bad shape, Liz. Your kidneys are failing."

My eyes widened, and I felt my cheek flush. "Of course," I thought, "how stupid of me not to have recognized the symptoms." I had contracted Chronic Fatigue Syndrome prior to leaving the UK, and I thought it was that. It never occurred to me that the dreaded Pylonephritis had returned. I wasted no time. I knew exactly what to do.

"I know what it is," I said, "and I know what I have to do."

I pulled myself up from the floor and beat as hasty a retreat as I could to get to my apartment, leaving them with their mouths hanging open. I crawled up my stairs on all fours. I did that when no one was looking. I continued, breathlessly, across the bedroom carpet. I was wracking my brain. Where was Fr. Anselm's phone number? Where would it be? Surely, I still had it somewhere. An old address book from the UK, maybe? I was panicked and exhausted from the shock and all, so I reached up from the floor and grabbed the handle on the drawer of my bedside table. I tugged and rolled out of the way. Mercifully, the drawer flew out, slamming to the floor and tossing the contents everywhere. I started to rummage through them when I saw, lying close by, my tiny address book with its gold cover that used to live in my purse. It had flipped open to the very page I needed, with Fr. Anselm's name and number right there. I froze. That was freaky! I began to shake at the obvious confirmation that I had to get hold of Fr. Anselm and that the dread sickness had returned. But, dear God, he was as old as Methuselah six years before. Please don't let him be dead. Surely he was, but I had to try.

I called. He answered the phone! On a Sunday! Unheard of!

"Fr. Anselm," I said, "you won't remember me but…"

I was interrupted with an exasperated, "Oh, hush, child, of course, I remember you. You're Elizabeth, and what I want to know is why you have been in my masses every day for the past six months?" Oh, Lord!

"I'm so sorry, Father; I got sick again."

"I knew it! I told you! I warned you!"

"I'm so sorry. I'll come back immediately."

"You will do no such thing," he snapped. "You will stay there, and you will find a priest there."

"But I don't know where to find one", I started to say.

Again, back he came with, "There have to be Carmelites there. Find them. There will be somebody. These Americans, they're not St. Teresa's, of course, but they'll have to do. Just do as I say."

"Yes, Father, of course I will." Before another word could be spoken, he was gone.

It was later explained to me that there are two factions amongst the Carmelites, the Discalced branch embracing the spirituality of St. Teresa of Avila and the others who embrace St. Therese of Lisieux, commonly known as Little Flower because of her simple, childlike way to Jesus. Both are Doctors of the Church. Both are terrific, in their own way. So what's up with these men!

I pulled out the telephone directory and found the Carmelites. I called, and I called, and I called with mounting frustration. I was certain that somebody would be there on a Sunday, but that is actually the very day that they are least likely to be available. Don't expire on a Sunday, people! The priests are either celebrating masses or having a well-deserved meal with friends. I just kept calling when, suddenly, and by now unexpectedly, a light, musical voice said, "Our Lady of Mount Carmel Church. Fr. Tom Alkire speaking. Can I help you?"

I was gob stopped. Oh, Lord, a priest! Suddenly, I didn't know what to say because the story was so bizarre. I wasn't ready.

"Ah", I said, "I really don't know. I need a priest, but an ordinary one won't do." Not exactly the best way to win him over, but I pushed on. "I need a priest who understands certain things for I have a strange story, and I desperately need help."

"What kind of things, my dear?"

What is it with these priests and that darned "my dear"?

"Forgive me, this is extremely embarrassing to me," I stammered. "I'm talking of dark forces, Father."

"Ah, well then, I'm your man," he said. "I have some knowledge of such things."

What were the chances of that? With what I now know, they were slim to none! Only God! "What seems to be the problem?" he asked.

I suggested he call Fr. Anselm, which he did, and he called me back after their conversation.

"I have spoken with my brother priest, and he has filled me in on what took place with you in London. I am not an appointed exorcist in this Diocese, so I will need permission from the Bishop. It should take about a week."

"A week?" I screeched. "I'm very, very sick."

"Yes, you are," he replied. "Shall we make an appointment for a week from tomorrow, then? Good. All being well, I'll see you then."

And so it was. I walked into his miniscule office and was confronted by a veritable giant. He was six foot six and big with it, about my own age, and he was wielding a ridiculous miniature watering can over a wilting plant hanging from the ceiling.

"Come along in, my dear. Take a seat and make yourself comfortable. I'll be right with you," he said, in an upbeat, cheerful voice.

I was sick, but I wasn't dead, and the contrast between this great hulk and the frail Fr. Anselm was not lost on me. I had to smile. For some obscure reason, I thought I'd finally met my match. "I'm done," I was thinking, "I won't have my way with this man." As if I'd had my way with Fr. Anselm! Weird. I didn't even know what I meant. It was a strange sensation, yet I was intrigued. He glanced my way and said, "My, my, you are dying, aren't you."

"Why do you say so?" I asked.

"Your nose is bright green, corruption setting in." Nice, I thought, but at least he really was one of the weird ones, exactly what I needed. I sat down and commenced to light up, since there was an ashtray by my chair, asking while I did so, "Mind if I smoke?"

"Oh, if you must," he said, conjuring up a small cough on cue.

"It can be my penance."

"Oh, good!" I said. "Happy to help out," not having a clue what he was talking about! We were off to a running start and had the measure of each other right up front. Neither of us had seen anything like the other in our entire lives. We were to spend many extraordinary years in combat, and not always on the same side; sometimes he was on his, and sometimes I found the guts to be on mine.

Unexpectedly, and in the same tone of voice, he said, "I'm afraid you're not going to have your healing, my dear."

"What?" I asked, shocked. "What on earth do you mean? Why not?"

"My Lord says no. He gave you an invitation last time, and you turned him down. This time you have to do it his way, or you won't be healed."

"What on earth are you talking about?" I asked, getting really upset and beginning to feel duped. "Who said that? What Lord? I didn't hear anything."

"The Lord Jesus," he said.

"Who?" I blurted out.

"Jesus." he replied.

Oh, this was becoming altogether too much. "Are you a real priest?" I asked.

"Yes, yes, I can provide all the particulars if you give me a moment to go to my cell."

"That won't be necessary," I said, thinking to myself, we've got a right one here who maybe should be in a cell! The old priest never mentioned any Jesus.

"Isn't he a mythological character, that Jesus?"

"Oh, no, no, no, my dear, not at all. He's alive and well."

"How can that be? How do you know that?"

"For many reasons," he said, "not least because he lives in me."

"Lives in you?" I asked, very quietly, tiptoeing gently, in case he was off his rocker.

"Yes," he said. "That's how I know he's not ready to heal you."

"But you said you could deliver me today."

"I did, but he says no, and he's the Boss." Somehow, I knew that he was speaking the truth. I just knew.

After a little more discussion, I heard myself say, "If this Jesus is real, and apparently he is, I am in terrible trouble. What do I have to do?" He looked me straight in the eye with such a mixture of joy, compassion and love that I squirmed with embarrassment. (What I didn't know was that the Sunday liturgy had been on the rich young man who asked the very same question!). I had never seen anything like that look.

When I questioned him about it, he said, "That's Jesus looking at you through my eyes. He loves you very much." Oh, help! "How can he?" I asked, "He doesn't even know me."

He just smiled. "So, back to your question, what are you to do? You in particular?" He paused. "You will have to give up everything. You are called to follow him all the days of your life and to serve him." Golly! He saw my hesitation, for I didn't really understand what he was asking of me and, what's more, I didn't want to!

He asked, "Have you any children?"

"Yes, a daughter, in college in London."

"Do you love her?"

"Immensely."

"Do you want her to have the kind of life you have had."

"Never."

"Then," he said, "Jesus is the only way to ensure it. I understand from the Spirit that you come from an evil lineage, and the rot needs to stop right here, with you, to protect those coming after you. To give them, and you, a chance at life. Will you do it?"

With no more ado, I replied, "For my daughter, I will do it."

I knew nothing of what he spoke, but my gut told me it was true, and I had better do it, without the vaguest notion as to why I knew. I just did. I had to do whatever he said to do, not only to save my physical life but also to save my child from something even more sinister. There was no time to wait until I understood. I was out of time with no more chances. The dye was cast. I just had to do it, whatever it was.

At my "yes" to Jesus, the priest embarked immediately on the "healing", as he preferred to call it. We talked some more, and he questioned me to ensure that I was in agreement with all that Fr. Anselm had told him of the previous affair. He sat at his desk, and I sat opposite him, holding his big, strong hands. That was comforting. He began to pray.

"I'm sorry to butt in," I said, fearfully, "I really don't think English will do for this," doubting that he was up to the job! Sorry, folks, if I'm offending you, but my life was in the balance here.

"The old priest used Latin," I added.

"Did he, though? Well, I do a fair job in Spanish," he replied, "I could use that."

I realized that I had piqued his pride, and he was retaliating with mockery. He didn't understand the extent of my fear, although it wouldn't have taken the brain of Britain to work it out. I rose up and blurted out, "I think that remark was beneath both of us."

He looked sheepish, had the grace to apologize, and tried again with, "What about this then?" as he went into some other language.

I listened for a moment and said, with relief, "That sounds fine. That will do nicely, thank you," and I settled down.

Unknown to me, he was using the gift of tongues, his heavenly language (1 Corinthians 12:7-11). No wonder it was perfect! This time there was no manifestation from me whatsoever, as there had been on the previous occasion. When he had finished praying the fever had gone. Just like that! I was weak, tired, but I felt well. There was no sickness, and I knew it. I was healed! I never returned to the hospital; there was no need.

Fr. Tom was a rare breed. His deep devotion to Mary's intercession and the precious blood of Jesus, as well as the power of the Holy Spirit and his gifts, made Father's prayer powerful enough to deliver me from that deadly kidney disease. I have been free of it from that day to this, twenty-six years later. Jesus uses his apostles to heal now just as he did when he walked the earth with them.

Fr. Anselm offered me the institutional Church, which, to me, was a cold, dark place. Fr. Tom offered me the man Jesus, fully human, fully divine, and his living, vibrant, breathing Family. No contest. By receiving Jesus and surrendering my life, I came into a new life and a new way of understanding it. I left this world, as I knew it, and entered the Kingdom of God, a whole other world with nothing else on earth like it. I went into the priest's office close to death. A couple of hours later, and my physical life was saved; my soul was saved, and now I was fixated on one thing and one thing only: the work of the Lord. I was born again, born from above spiritually (John 3:1-12). I started a brand new life that day, a fresh start. I had a future to look forward to instead of lingering death. What a turn of events!

CHAPTER SIX
AN UNKNOWN WORLD

F r. Tom was really something else. Not only was he ahead of his time, with an eerie ability to sniff out the Holy Spirit, but he took a whole lot of flak regarding his message and methods. I'm not sure why. Maybe it was that no one person should be expected to have to embrace all of what he taught, and believed to be essential, and I don't know that he did expect it. I just know he wanted it. He certainly hoped they would. After all, the Church is vast, with room for many varying viewpoints, which in one way is good, but, in another, can make unity difficult. The book of Ephesians was our "little Bible" and I, for one, learned to live it. If you're curious, I will tell you what he taught me, but, as in all things with this book, just jump the bits that don't interest you to something that does. A quarter of a century ago, Fr. Tom adjured me to live the following if I wanted to be a true Christian, which means, of course, being a true disciple. This is his take:

- We must be born from above to enter the Kingdom of heaven.
- We must be rooted and grounded in The Word.
- We must receive the Baptism in the Holy Spirit and his charismatic gifts.
- We must lay on hands for healing of all kinds, especially and including the inner child.
- We must make our Consecration to the Immaculate Heart of Mary, in full trust that she will lead us to Jesus.

- We must wear the Brown Scapular and fervently pray the rosary.
- We should have devotion to the Holy Angels, day in and out, especially our Guardian.
- We should live in communities of priests and lay alike, to share together the life.
- We knew to call on the name of Jesus and his most precious blood when in need, which was all the time!
- Eucharistic Adoration, daily Mass and regular Reconciliation were essential.
- We knew that the Traditions and the Magisterium were the last word.
- We were to be grateful and rejoice in all things.
- We were to learn to be honest and sincere with self, God and each other.
- Every decision was to be prayed through and referred to the Holy Spirit before action was taken
- We had to learn the ways of Spirit Warfare for our own protection and the deliverance of others.
- Fasting, tithing, donating and giving alms.

All of this we were to do in order to make our faith a way of life and to turn us into warriors for Jesus and Mary, fully armed.

All of this I learned, and learned to do, at Fr. Tom's feet in the years we were together and, of course, I continue to live it to the best I can. It was hard, rigorous training, but he was right. I have needed it all, and it has taken my entire commitment to achieve, but it was essential if I were to do what I'm called to do. Can others do it this way? I've no idea. Only if they feel called, I suppose, and I did, and I was. The Lord went to a lot of trouble to put me together with Fr. Tom. He really uses his priests in a very precise way. I was truly blessed and had much inner healing; but let me tell you, people, the Sacrament of Reconciliation got me more healed and probably more loved than any other form of prayer. If you hurt, I mean really hurt, go there! But go with repentance, not just confession. If you find a warm confessor, be blessed, but don't worry about it. Jesus in the Sacrament is what heals and sets you free. I remember protesting about some crusty old priest, who was less than helpful, when Jesus popped up with, "Why did you go to Confession?"

"Hello, Lord," close to tears, "to get absolution from the Church for my sins."

"Did you get it?" he asked.

"I did."

"So, why complain? Be glad. He's old but you got what you came for."

Amen!

Despite Fr. Tom's brothers not being particularly open to his charismatic leanings, he didn't let that stop him. We, his few followers, were not exactly popular with priests or parishioners, either, but what can you do? When God convicts, he convicts, and he convicted me that I was to eat and swallow all of the above, daunting though it was. When I asked Fr. Tom why he believed I was to follow this route, he said:

"Because it's what I know. If God didn't want you to know what I know then he should have sent you to a different priest instead of half way around the world to me."

That made sense; so from then on, I just got on with it and took the brickbats. He'd been in Houston from Chicago only two weeks when I called the Monastery for help and he answered the phone. Surely, that was no coincidence. I gave up my life to his regime of "work, study and prayer", even although I also had a demanding full time job. I threw myself into the teachings wholeheartedly, trusting and obeying. We hit it off well enough to get the job done, despite interesting, and often painful, personality quirks on both parts. We truly were the odd couple!

The good news of Jesus can be very bad news, indeed, for a woman of the world with an independent streak, and it fell to Fr. Tom to get me where I wanted to go, which was to fulfill God's perfect will for my life. I was so intrigued by the notion that God had a perfect plan for each one of us that I couldn't let it alone. Curiosity was killing me to know mine. Can you imagine? Jesus knows you so well and loves you so much that he knows exactly and precisely what will make you your most happy, then sets about wanting to help you to get it. That was irresistible to me, so I left everything to hunt it down. In October 1982, I walked out of my life and into his, and never left, although there were times I wanted to! It's not the first time I was heading to the airport if he didn't stop me! Painful though it has been, and whose life isn't, without question, it's the greatest way of life there is because it is the Life. This life of mine is the fullness of life with a capital "L". I have never been more fulfilled, satisfied and more hopeful than I am today.

Fr. Tom's role was to Christianize me, and it was a major task for both of us. We had so much to learn about each other's worlds. He'd never before had to train an atheist coming in out of the cold, and, with the pride of a Catholic, he found it almost impossible to believe that anyone could be totally ignorant of Christ and his Church. There are so many Catholics, and the Church has been around for so many years, that it simply doesn't occur to them that anyone could know nothing of their culture or their faith. To my knowledge, I'd never met a Christian. Some say I could have, unwittingly, but true Christians can't be hidden, can they? There's just something about them. It will show in some way or another, don't you think? We're just different: annoying, delightful or whatever, but different. I'm thinking that the most wonderful woman I ever met, authoritative, wise and very kind, was French Mauritian and Catholic. I do believe that Madame Mayer was a true Christian. I loved her greatly. I encountered various brands of Catholicism in my travels, but none of it grabbed me, probably because nobody could tell me why they were Catholic or even why they went to Church. They just said that I should. We need to change that! We have to have a reason that makes sense to others. They are missing out on a good thing if we don't tell them!

After my first meeting and healing, Fr. Tom packed me off with a bunch of books and instruction to read them, to write down what I didn't understand and to call him when I was done. One week later, I called. He was cold.

"I believe you were to read the books I gave you."

"I have," I said, surprised at his manner and a little miffed.

"And what about the notes I wanted?"

"I took notes, Father. I did exactly what you said. I told you that I would."

"My goodness, then you'd better get down here."

I did. He thumbed through some of the notes and looked disturbed.

"You really don't know anything, do you?" he asked.

I shook my head and gripped my lip. "I told you."

I was troubled that he might not have time for me but all he said was, "We've a lot of work to do and no time to be lost."

I wondered about that but let it go. He instructed me, talked with me, prayed with me every day for six weeks, and then announced that I was ready to go and live in a Christian community.

"What?" I asked, perplexed. "You're sending me away?"

"I have to, my dear, you need to be with Christians who can teach you the ropes, lay hands on you daily and pray with you. With the work we've done, you will pass as one of them now that you are born into your new life and have received the Baptism of the Holy Spirit that Jesus brought to us (John 1:34). You have received Christ and opted for his service. They will take you to the next stage."

"And what is that?" I asked him, "And how long will I be there?"

"How long is a piece of string?" he replied.

I was stunned, and fear gripped me. I felt betrayed, or abandoned, perhaps even rejected. I don't know; it just felt horrible being sent away. "Why can't I stay here?" I pleaded.

"You need to be in a household where all in that particular place have given up everything to live the life so that they have nothing else on their minds but serving the Lord and those he sends. You have many needs, my dear, that cannot be met here. It is the joy of these Communities to embrace new Christians.

I was even more perplexed. "Are you not Christians, here, then?" I asked, in all innocence.

"Yes, of course we are. You are just not ready for the Church, but you did respond to Jesus. You need to be cocooned in the ways of the Lord. These fine people at Redeemer will be able to build on what I have taught you and get you off to a good start. God has work for you." And that was that.

Fifteen minutes away was the ecumenical Christian community of the Church of the Redeemer, Episcopal, an inner city church where I was to spend fifteen months of my life. The pastor was the Rev. Jeff Schiffmayer, and I liked him tremendously. He was a family man who obviously loved his wife and kids. He was gentle and pensive with a little smile that played around his lips as he communed with the God he loved. Fr. Tom kept hounding me to get into that community, so I called and called to speak with Jeff without success. His wife must have wanted to strangle me for calling so often! There was a screening system for newcomers to discern if God wanted them there. A household had to be found, and then Jeff had to interview the newcomer. All I remember of mine was that he told me to find a church near my apartment and go there. Well, that annoyed me, didn't it, after making all that effort.

I retorted, "What's the use of that when I don't know what brand of Christianity I'm supposed to be in? Here, you just have Jesus and the Holy Spirit, and that's what I need."

He smiled. He liked that, but by this time I was kicking myself for fighting so hard to get into a place where I didn't want to be! I was so scared. The other thing he liked was when I said I didn't want to be with people who were pious in their piety. His eyes crinkled with silent laughter, and I was in. They were ordinary, down-to-earth Christians at Redeemer, just my kind, but they had trouble placing me in a household.

I suspect they weren't falling over themselves to take in a Brit because it's hard enough initiating a newcomer without confronting massive cultural differences to boot. And don't kid yourselves, Brits; there are no two more foreign people around than you and the USA. We have a real struggle on our hands trying to relate and communicate, separated by a similar language as we are, and I'm still working at it. Mercifully, David and Eugenia Rust took a deep breath and said "yes," and I'm so glad they did. They had lived in the UK for a while, when David was flying, so I wasn't completely alien to them! Being in that community was the most enriching introduction to Christianity that I could ever have had, even though I thought it would kill me at the time. They did build on everything I had learnt from Fr. Tom, so there was no conflict there and, although I had brought a lot of emotional pain with me, we dealt with it head on, with love and prayer. It was everything a Christian community should be, with all its lumps and bumps. I will always be grateful for their kindness and patience as they broke me in.

My first mid-day prayer meeting was in the sanctuary with only half a dozen folks and nowhere to hide. What a motley crew we were. I was dying a million deaths of embarrassment and shame at being there at all, too complicated to explain at this point, and it worsened exponentially as the singing started. Dear God, have mercy! I never heard anything like it. There was an enormous bear of a man, sitting beside me, who had been through some stuff, for it marked his face, literally. He looked like he'd been beaten and dragged from every bar in town, and some, and a massive scar ripped brow to chin to prove it. He had a mass of black hair with a beard to match and a voice that rumbled like a volcano. And the size of him, dear Lord! He terrified me. I mean, really. I couldn't breathe for being beside him. After the pathetic "singing," my face was scarlet, for them, for God, for me! The big, black bear turned his head to look me square on, started his rumble till it erupted into laughter, his face creasing with joy and said, very slowly and distinctly, "Make a joyful noise unto the Lord!"

I was stunned for a second, and then I cracked up and couldn't stop laughing. We were firm friends from that day on. I called him Joyful Noise because that's exactly what he was, and he loved it. He had a heart of gold did Joyful Noise, and his friendship for my daughter and I warms me to this day. When she and I left the community, for she came for a short time, he hand-painted two mugs with our names in hearts and presented them with real sadness that we were leaving. He was the epitome of Redeemer: always expect the unexpected! The Episcopalian priests were good men all, but I could see the exhausting challenge in trying to keep two families happy. Being married made them more approachable than Catholic priests, especially for women, but, on the other hand, they were torn in a way that our priests are not. Celibacy is such a great gift that I enjoy to the max, but I know it's a call because I would never have chosen it. In fact, I gave up the man I loved to obey that call. The right marriage is wonderful, too. Everything under God turns out great, let's face it, if you give it long enough!

If I make Redeemer sound like Utopia, it's only in retrospect! I have made many decisions in the Lord that have cost me everything, every time, some more frightening than others, but going to Redeemer was tops on the terror scale. About six weeks after I heard the name of Jesus, I literally turned the key in the lock of my apartment, leaving most of my belongings, and drove my car, chock full to the brim, to the community, sight unseen and heart in mouth. I didn't know if I would be wearing navy knickers to the knees and scrubbing floors at 4.00 a.m. before getting to my day job, or what. I had never attended a church service, there or anywhere. When I questioned Fr. Tom about what would be required of me, his only remark was, "No idea. You'll find out when you get there."

Thanks a lot. I expected not to have my cigarettes, but I sprinkled my room with them just the same to prove I wasn't deprived. More like depraved, huh! I could smoke outside and have my evening Scotch, but I wasn't comfortable doing that either, so I refrained, cold turkey. Ouch! I wasn't prepared for no television, fun, laughter or enjoyable conversation in the evenings. The Rusts were quiet, very, very quiet. We each had our little lamp and our books until it was time for bed. Because I had a day job and paid a little into the household, my duties were light for which I was extremely grateful. Nevertheless, for all that, it was a long six months. At that point, I had sufficiently established myself as to be allowed to room with my dear and delightful friend, Merilee Koss, my first convert. Merilee was Jewish, funny, and deeply hurt. I was hurt, too. Unresolved hurts have a way of getting in the way of relationships, and so we parted company, sadly. I miss her still. I really loved her. She went to Israel. I grin when I think of her because she was so much more fun than I was at the time. My free spirit had been locked up by then, so I must have been a pain. God bless Merilee, and her kids, wherever she is.

The writing was on the wall that I would be leaving Redeemer.

Two things stand out in my mind. I suppose I'd been there about five months when I attended the Mother's Day service (the services were beyond words beautiful with George Mims at the musical helm). As people were praying thanksgiving for their mothers I thought that was nice, but mine wasn't any great shakes, so I thought I would give thanks for Jesus' mother instead, especially in view of what she had done for me. I proclaimed boldly, "God bless Jesus' mother, Mary." It fell like a stone on concrete.

Eugenia, my housemother, turned to me with arms spread wide and said softly, "Oh, Liz," as she buried my head in her chest. Evidently, they were not big on Mary! I had committed a heinous gaffe, unwittingly, for there was devotion to Mary in the St. Augustine prayer book that I found in their bookstore. Go figure! However, what had I done wrong, really, when you think about it? How could they not love Jesus' Mother, though they could give a shout out for their own? How could Jesus not love the mother who carried Him physically within her for nine solid months giving him of her very flesh and blood, communicating with him in the silence of her heart for weeks, months and even years, in and out of the womb? Everything Jesus knew in his earthly state she taught him, and she stood by him through thick and thin. How could he not want to move heaven and earth for his mother, the maiden chosen by his Father? How could he want a heaven without her? It's not only unthinkable but, to my mind, it's ridiculous not to consider that Mary is just as alive as is her Son. Think of all her apparitions and visits from heaven to earth! Who knows the earthly Jesus better than she does? I reckon we owe her a mighty vote of thanks. Only God knows what she went through to get Jesus to where he needed to be for our sakes.

The second time I knew I would have to go from Redeemer was at a meeting, along with others, presided over by some of the priests and elders. I was having a difficult time trying to find my "place", whatever that was, in a new world in which I had found myself. I wanted to go back to the beginning, to find the origins of the Church, to know where Jesus' people were, so I asked, "Where is the church of Christ?"

"I believe there's one down the road," one said.

"No, no," I jumped in, "I mean the original people that were with Jesus when He left the world and went back to heaven, the people He left his church with, or their descendants, you know? Where are they? Do I have to go to Jerusalem?"

They looked from one to another, pondering, and then someone spoke up: "She must mean the Catholic Church."

"No," I screamed internally, surely not. I couldn't mean that, could I?

"It's been here since the beginning," he said, "since Peter, and it's still here, isn't it, so that must be what she means."

"Are you sure?" I asked.

"If you mean Mary Magdalene and Peter, James and John and all of these, then, yes, they were the ones he left to carry on his work."

I stared at them, brow furrowed and puzzled, and said, "If you know that, then what are you all doing here? I've been counterfeit my whole life, one way or another, and now I'm seeking truth. If that's where the roots of the Church lie, then that's where I have to go, like it or not." And that was that. It's too long a story to tell you how Mary made it clear to me, supernaturally, of course, that she wanted me back at Mount Carmel, but she did, so that is where I went, back to Fr. Tom, no surprise there! He was the one whom she sent.

I cannot tell you how painful it was to leave the community I had come to love. Everyone was passionate about their lives and what God was saying to them in the Spirit, both individually and collectively, sharing involvement in every day affairs so that no one was left alone and with signs of love a daily happening. We lived the Scriptures and shared our tears and our joys. It was anguish going from that to what appeared to me to be drab, forgive me, brothers and sisters, dull, "religious" parish life, where most seemed to be secular people attending church rituals rather than people of the Spirit seeking truth and healing through Jesus. I had been with people who were striving for the courage to take risks to live the challenge of love, and now I was starting all over again with the Church I didn't want in the first place. The angst, the loss and pain of leaving the world system to enter the Redeemer community was now replaced by something even worse. I was truly, now, an alien in a very far and foreign land. I felt like I had gone from the promise of a blossoming new life into death and darkness, and I was alone in it.

Parish life talked of committees; community life talked of ministries. I had to learn yet another language. It seemed to me like nobody listened to anybody far less thinking to listen to God. I liked that people were family oriented, but they seemed to be blind to the bigger picture of God's family, where, if we take care of them ours is included in an exceptional way. I was accustomed to scripture being taught and discussed as a basic manual for living, a kind of "how to" book that gave me something solid to stand on, along with others, as we worked it out together. In parish life, I was alone; I was scared all over again. I have never felt so incredibly lonely. I was at a loss. I started asking around, and I visited a few other parishes only to discover that they were not much different. In addition, the music in some of them, oh, dear God, help us, and help our poor Jesus! I was encountering parish culture: that's just how it was at that time. And you know? That helped. It's just the way it was. I buried myself in Fr. Tom's teachings, the Sacraments, the Bible, much prayer and the heavenly family, just to be able to breathe.

I believe we're to have fun with what we're doing, whatever it is. I think we're supposed to enjoy being people, never mind being Christians. God so wants us to be happy! We're inclined to be somewhat legalistic or hard-nosed about what we think we're supposed to be doing, and we want so much to get it right. Instead, we should enjoy being absurdly, ridiculously loved, sharing our own individual, delightful thoughts and feelings about everything and anything, with others, and with one another. How good would it feel to be able to say, in a safe environment, everything that has been on our minds about God, The Church, Jesus and everything else that pertains, talking openly and freely, without fear of being jumped on? Wouldn't that be great! I feel that I need to interject here that I am not talking about the priests so much. The people most likely to crucify us over some small point are the laity. I remember well when I was God's unofficial, self-appointed police officer. I thought it was my job, and it was exhausting. He had to save me, and others, from me! We're here to learn, not to know. How can we learn anything if it's not safe to be wrong? We need to put away the old way, the childish thing, and learn to speak up without fear of condemnation. We need to stop with the finger-wagging eyes. Be wrong! It's so personally validating to admit you are exactly who you are, with all your faults and failings and with all your good stuff and to enjoy finding that out. You're as much right as you are wrong, and who cares anyway except you. You are your own life's journey! Why don't we try taking Jesus and his teachings a lot more seriously and ourselves a whole lot less! We would laugh a whole lot more, that I do know!

Yet still, slowly, the new way is catching on, more with some priests than with others, certainly, and the same with the laity. Radical Love is seeking apostles for the end time, a remnant, bringing the fire and zeal of Elijah. John Paul II was an incredible example. Now, there was a Peter for the hour, baptized in the Holy Spirit, tongue speaking, charismatic lover of Mary. He understood her essential role in the second coming of Christ, united with her spouse the Holy Spirit, to prepare a place for the return of our King Jesus. Now we have Pope Benedict XVI preaching his beautiful message of love! Would you not say that he, also, is preparing us for the return of the King, when all that will remain is peace, love and joy?

Vatican II came in like a lion and sent us scurrying for the sheepfold. However, the gentle breeze in its wake is penetrating the hearts and minds of enough truth-seekers, layer by layer, until we become light for the Kingdom. There will be a new understanding of a message given long ago. Our Father sent the Virgin Mary to Fatima with a strong, prophetic message in 1917 that we must turn back to God. But what did we do? Those who even bothered to listen did not take her seriously, or her prophecy of terrible wars and the rise of Communism, which did happen just as she forewarned. He then sent the Holy Spirit at Vatican II, in the 1960's, to wake us up. Are we making the same mistake again? Are we not listening, again? When I came into the Church in the early Eighties, there was nothing but confusion, and all I heard was "pre-Vat and post-Vat", and I knew nothing of either one. More and more I turned for clarity to the woman who was there from the beginning and continued to show up throughout the ages: Mary. I studied her messages in her apparitions approved by the Church at the same time as I studied scripture and Church teaching, and nowhere did I find conflict or discrepancy. On the contrary, she kept me steady, so I let her teach me. One day it will hit us just what the Holy Spirit wanted changed in the Church at Vatican II after the many doubts, fears and factions have been put to rest. Here's the question for each one of us to consider, whose voice are we listening to? There's the devil, God, each other, and ourselves. Whose voice is predominant in your life?

Renewed Catholics, in the light of the Holy Spirit and the heart of Mary, are new wineskins to hold the fresh new wine of the new way. They will love the Church, and more, in the fullness of what she has been given, no longer peering through a glass darkly in dulled obedience, but fully alive to the call of the Kingdom. For them, everything will become brand new, for those risk-takers who are willing to step out and prepare for the King's return. Jesus showed us a New Way to live, and he longs for us to be doing it. When he asked if he would find any faith at all on his return, I believe he was speaking of this day. He will be looking for faith communities living out the first century church in the way that he left it, with signs and wonders: healing the sick, raising the dead, driving out demons and setting the captives free from all of the sin and pain of this world (Mark 16:17). Where are we, brothers and sisters? Will he visit your parish? Are we doing what Jesus did, and more? John Paul II, a handpicked Pope for this hour, told us what is needed. A New Pentecost! A New Evangelization! A New Springtime! When did you last do something new with your faith, beloved? When you do, God will.

It's all in the Word! When we ask the Holy Spirit to enlighten us as we read it, he does, and he strengthens us and teaches us how to live it and how to pray through it. After all, he wrote it! We need to rip that Word apart and devour it (Rev 10:9) if we are to become the holy people we are called to be, in order to stand firm for what is to come. Rise up, lay people, really learn to pray, to worship, to storm the gates of heaven and take your place alongside our beleaguered priests. Unite your gifts and bring life to your parish. Church should never, never be boring but in so many places it is, to the point of atrophy! I love the Church! I care deeply about us! I have been blessed and healed by priests, and I have been crushed by priests, until there was nothing left but Jesus! The truth of that makes me laugh aloud. Why does truth do that, I wonder? I guess it makes us laugh when it does not make us cry. All is good. God uses his priests, that I know! Just love them! Oh, another suggestion - take your complaints to heaven; it works! God knows! He hears and understands. God really gets it!

CHAPTER SEVEN
PRIEST FOR ALL SEASONS

Some of us don't know what to think about the body of Christ these days. There is so much wrong with it, yet so much right with it, that it's a challenge to sort it all out, especially in light of the many Christian TV programs that present a different viewpoint. If you're solid in your Catholic faith, they can be enlightening and helpful, but if you're not, they can confound, as if we're not confused enough since Vatican II. The challenge in this new day is to find a place for yourself in the Church where you can serve, a place that works for you, as an individual, where you can bring your gifts and talents. This may no longer be news to you, but you could certainly be excused for wondering why all of us are now being asked to serve in the Church, without exception? In the past, anyone who heard a call from God or was attracted to him in some way became priests and nuns. There wasn't anywhere else to go with it, so they served the Church in schools, missions etc. And God was happy. And the people were happy. Everybody knew his place and knew what to do.

Then God.......! Only he knew when he planned to rupture through time and space with the astonishing news of the imminent return of his Son: Vatican II was the bolt from the blue. That was when he read our mail and said 'get ready'. Maybe we didn't recognize that Vatican II was all about that, but the Holy Spirit is so gentle, and we are so slow, that he gives us time to move into a new understanding. It's not so much that we're late. It comes down to whether we are listening now, whether we are open to accepting now? Have we got beyond our initial fear at what took place in the

Church forty years ago and know that it is safe to breathe again, realizing that much good came of it? Not least, for me, is that we are no longer a faceless "glob" called "The Church" but we are a mass of vibrant, fascinating, opinionated, talented people who make up that glob called the Church. It's not a membership club but a community with everyone playing a wonderful, enjoyable part, learning to live together with joy and full acceptance. Mind you, people still ask me if I'm a nun. They're stuck in the old way of thinking. They work it out that because I'm totally in love with Jesus and Mary that I must be married to the Church. In reality, I'm married to Jesus and serve him in a different way, through the Church!

This is what he says to us, "Come and rest awhile. Sit with me. Tell me all about it—your fears, your troubles. What do you want to know? Ask me. Tell me what you want. Do not tell me what you do not want. What are you up to in life? What do you feel about it? How can I help you? I have all kinds of solutions to offer if you give me the time to work it through with you. I do not want you to be alone! I love you too much to see you struggle alone. Have friends, beloved. If, sadly, there are none, turn to me. I am here. I make a very good friend." Isn't that beautiful? That's how he speaks to us. That's his heart for us. There is no one kinder when we slip and fall, when we're hurt and lost. Now that he's preparing to return, he wants us to know him in ordinary ways. That's why he came down, so that we would know him through one another. He wants us to be available for the work he calls us to do and to enjoy our lives. Can you help him? Will you? All he needs are humble, joyful people, from all walks of life and persuasions, who are open to his friendship.

I love seeing what God is up to in his Church, in my life, and in yours! I just love it! It's what keeps me alive! We're so blessed to be Catholics, not only because of the Eucharist, but also because of the Magisterium, the sacred teaching of the Church. Centuries of believing and praying have nailed down the truth of the teachings until we are certain of God's heart and mind regarding his Church, his people. If we follow that truth, we are the safest people on earth, safe from the devil, from others and from our own foolishness and ourselves! The Church has surely been our mother, and Mary, as

Mother of the Church, will lead us to the very heart of her Son. Jesus will never again dirty his hands on Satan. The privilege has been given to Mary's heel(Gen 3: 15) as the new, pure Eve, reversing Eden's curse. She will use the Church. She will use the true priesthood, birthed and anointed by Christ himself, and the latter-day lay apostles, whom she, herself, has raised up. And we will be victorious! God never abandons what he started, and he started this Church!

I wonder why some of us rail against tradition? Too much of anything isn't good, but why pick on tradition. Say what you like about it, but if it's so bad, why do millions troop around the ancient ruins of Europe, year after year, seeking roots? Why has genealogy become big business? Why do adopted or deserted people seek their biological parents if roots don't matter? It's in us to want to know, don't you think? People want roots, and the Catholic Church has them, deep and strong. Our other Christian brothers and sisters are presently represented by some 26,000 denominations, or so I'm told, all of which sprouted from our branches beginning only four hundred years ago. They're new to the game compared to our one Catholic Church of two thousand years. Mother Church is wise enough to allow dissensions within her branches, but she has parameters! As with all good mothers, we know just how far we can go before we are treading dangerous waters! Do others have that safety net to help rein them in? I'm glad we do. We're kids and we do get carried away with ourselves, don't we.

Let me show you just how far some priests will go to turn us loose for Jesus. Take my Fr. Anselm, an old-time priest with a life of hidden suffering. He kept his gift inside the cloisters and ministered to the ones God sent. On the other hand, we have Fr. Tom, a pre-Vatican II priest who stayed the course to learn the new way, wrestling the bear to the ground until it registered, God bless him. That was no mean feat for his legalistic brain! He held me under water, only letting me up to help others, until I could swim without coercion and train others in the way! That's the call of the laity! Passing it on! Teaching each other! It takes a lot of strength, a lot of power, and an awful lot of authentic love to endure the kind of suffering that births others into the Kingdom. It wasn't enough that

I become a good Church member through formation, which is essential. I had to be transformed from disciple to apostle, and the Holy Spirit led Fr. Tom to the very way to do it. There is a little book, *In the End My Immaculate Heart Will Triumph, consecration preparation for the Triumphant Victory of the Immaculate Heart of Mary,* published by Queenship Publishing. That's how I did it, that, coupled with Mary's "To my Beloved Priests", and added to my list of "doings", taught me the way of death to self. I started it in 1994 and have been praying and living it ever since. You might think that Fr. Tom was hard on me, but keep in mind that he knew from the "get-go" that I had a mission to fulfill. Note, also, that I was a pretty wild woman! I'd been charging around the world to very obscure places without a great deal of thought, if any at all. Who's been to Nouakchott, for heaven's sake? If you're wondering where that is, it's the capital of Mauritania. Where's that? Good question: Sahara Desert, Continent of Africa. Now you see that pinning me down for the Lord was no small task! That priest had to exercise every spiritual gift and power he had, which was considerable, to lead me from the darkness of this world into the light of the Kingdom of God. I am indebted to him and his Lady for the privilege of true discipleship. There's nothing like it, and there's nothing better. I really love my life. Never did before!

After seven years together, Father was called to another Parish. I remained in Carmel for eight more years when I was given another extraordinary Mentor. Dr. William Graham, Psychologist, lover of God and mankind, agreed to work with me. Bill had been twenty-five years a Holy Cross priest, and before that a Chemical Engineer, prior to his call to Psychology, so the Lord sent me a man for all seasons to round me out! As a priest and teacher, he had served in the missions in India and had loved it all. However, he had also loved a woman from afar, for more years than most people stay married! Finally, his brothers heard the voice of God that it was time for Bill to leave the priesthood, with permission and in good standing, which meant everything to him, and he was free to marry his beloved wife! Thank God that Bill followed his heart, for I cannot imagine what would have become of me without his particular love and skills. No one else could have given me what I needed at that time. Fr. Tom and I prayed two years for him to show up. Without Bill Graham, no one would ever have heard of me. His gentle, wise, born again, priestly self, combined with his knowledge of psychology, led me into the psycho-spiritual work I had been called to do. Jesus uses all of his men, and he uses them specifically.

Fr. Robert DeGrandis, a charismatic Jesuit, was in and out of my life with his powerful gifts. In the early days, he occasionally ministered with a woman and, worse yet, hang on to your hats, she wasn't Catholic! Shocking! That was so much fun! Betty Tapscott is an evangelical author/preacher in her own right who, apart from being helpful to me, personally, with words of knowledge, together with Fr. Bob gave a lot of hope for broken, hurting people. At one of their seminars, I stood in line for the anointing, yet again. I was always hoping for something to happen to lift the darkness within, a zap of something, anything, not to feel so left out of life. I was desperate. I was lost. I hurt, and the Lord wasn't showing up! I'd been sprinkled, dunked, sat on, pushed, pulled, shouted at and whispered at and still nothing! I had "received" the Baptism of the Holy Spirit over and over and over again with no apparent result, so I guessed I hadn't received it at all. Or had I? I've no idea. I just kept going after it, no matter who said what or what I looked like, despite my considerable vanity. We were so hungry for the things of God back then, just starving. I wish we were still. Anyway, there we were, all in rows, as Fr. Bob charged down the line anointing foreheads. It was my turn. Nothing! He moved on, stopped, looked back and saw me still standing. Back he came. Oh, boy.

"Elizabeth", he sighed, "you're resisting."

Aw, come on, Father, I was thinking, give me a holy break. Here I was, bursting a gut for release into the Spirit, and this was what I got.

"Don't think so, Father," I said, trying to be respectful, but wanting to crown him one.

"You're resisting. Surrender. Give it up. Just let go!"

Let go what? I was screaming inside. "Right," I thought, "if that's what you want then that's what you'll get." I'd been an actress. I knew how to fall to the floor. You want me to pretend? Then fine! I'll pretend and see where that gets us! I nodded, and he touched me again. I released my knees and fell. I lay there. And lay there. After a while, I heard the call for lunch break. I lay there. People stepped over me on their way out, and two hours later they stepped over me on their way back. I still lay there. I was glued to the floor and couldn't move a limb under the power of the Holy Spirit. I'm reminded of a little boy of about nine who came to one of my prayer meetings, with his Grandma. He came forward for the anointing and went down in the Spirit. When he got up he tugged on my sleeve and said, very seriously, "That thing wouldn't let me up."

I knew exactly how he felt. It's a strange business.

From time to time, Fr. Bob, as we called him then, would come to the Catholic Charismatic Center, in Houston. On this occasion, he called out that two people were walking with canes and that God wanted to heal them. I stood up and waved my cane in the air, anxious to get anything that was going.

"Come forward," he said. He laid hands on me and said, "Forgive everyone who's ever hurt you."

I did. It wasn't hard. I'd spent twenty years on it!

"Why are you using a cane?"

I told him that I was on steroids for Temporal Arteritis and Polymyalgia Rheumatica and had painfully stiff, swollen legs. He took my hand and started walking me when I added, "My hips hurt the most."

He kept on going, saying, "He's doing legs, not hips, legs."

Funny! I hobbled along, trying to keep up, when suddenly I called out, spontaneously and out of nowhere at all, "There it is!" The words just popped out of my mouth. Fr. Bob grinned wickedly and off we went, his chasuble flying and flapping as we charged around the huge sanctuary to wild applause. We stopped at the back as I panted for breath.

"Are you all right?" he asked.

Before I could say a thing, "There it is again!" popped out of the mouth again, and off we went again.

Talk about hilarious! Talk about exhilaration! It was wonderful! I was elated that my legs were healed; but on the way home I said, "Lord, what do you have against hips?"

He reminded me that a few days before, when asked what I would like from Jesus, I had said, "I used to enjoy curling up on a sofa with a good book, and my legs tucked under me. That would be nice."

That's exactly what I got. He was listening! Fr. Bob DeGrandis blessed me in so many ways with words of knowledge for inner healing and spiritual revelation that meant the world to me and helped propel me on my way.

I am indebted to Fr. William Wagner, ORC, a tall, handsome, American priest, whose call was to Opus Angelorum, or the Work of the Holy Angels, and who was based for many years in Fatima, Portugal. Fr. Tom Alkire had gone to great lengths to meet this priest so as to be consecrated to his Holy Angel and enrolled into that holy Work. Fr. Tom always liked to have a 'buddy' in his endeavors so he encouraged me to study for about three years that I, too, might be prepared to join in the wonderful work of the Angels. By being consecrated to them in this way, we are consecrated through them to God, as they carry out a special mission and ministry of grace in our lives. Interestingly, the very first scripture I received, on randomly opening a brand new bible, in 1982, was the following: "As St. Raphael (the Angel) explained to Tobit: "When you prayed, ...I brought a reminder of your prayers before the Holy One.... So now God sent me to heal you …….. I am Raphael, one of the seven holy angels who present the prayers of the saints and enter into the presence of the glory of the Holy One."[Tob 12:12, 14-15] Wasn't that great! Furthermore, the great Raphael has been with me ever since, along with my extraordinary Guardian Angel and his cohort, to say nothing of others. Perhaps there's a book in all the life-saving assistance I have had from my protectors, the holy angels. They are magnificent in their love for God. I was so privileged to be able to make my final pledge of service.

We flew to Fatima, well prepared. On arrival, we gathered with Fr. Wagner, along with a handful of others, for final instruction; then, around midnight, we walked, slowly, silently, towards the beautiful glassed-in shrine where Our Lady had appeared over a period of six months to three children: Lucia, Francisco and Jacinta.

The Angels preceded Mary's visits there, so it was perfect. It rained that night, softly and gently in the darkness, "a reminder of her sweet love and the presence of the Holy Spirit," I thought. The deceptively simple ceremony was performed, the flames of our candles reflecting back to us the dancing and flickering of our hearts in anticipation of the seriousness of the consecration we were about to make. It was an experience to be etched on my heart and soul for all eternity, in united mission.

Fr. Jozo Zovko, a Franciscan from Medjugorje, Croatia, where I journeyed several times, is another exceptional priest, exceptional in his gifts, exceptional in his love. His testimony ripped into my heart as he stood in front of a crowded church and announced, his eyes filled with tears and with riveting voice and posture, "I did not believe. I did not believe".

That, from a man who was imprisoned and tortured for his faith, for eighteen horrendous months, by the Communist regime. What did he not believe? He did not believe the villagers that Our Lady was appearing on the hillside, as she has done every day since, from January 1981 until the present time, and he was angry that the people were outside on the hill, instead of being in the church where he thought they ought to be. They were looking for Mary, it was true, and she was there. The reality of Father's pain at his disbelief in the apparition, years later, took me to a depth I had never known of what it is to love. During his private service, I was hit again in my heart, but with such a pain and such darkness within that I sobbed in despair. Fr. Jozo paid no attention, and that was all right, but his beautiful lady interpreter approached me.

"What's wrong?" she whispered.

"I don't know," I said. "Just anguish of soul." I told her, in passing, that I had been an atheist.

She threw her head back and said, "So was I. There is no worse hell. It is hell. Come!"

She guided me through the crowd to Fr. Jozo and told him. I have never, before or since, seen such a dazzling, rakish smile as his, radiant with the love of Jesus as he stretched his hands towards me, one on the front and one on the back, and he squeezed, I mean squeezed, with raw delight. Whatever it was, it left, right then, oh, yes. That's supernatural grace.

Fr.Jozo also came to the Catholic Charismatic Center. I was in a wheelchair and in much pain. I now had Fibromyalgia on top of everything else, but I was in good spirits. At the end of his talk, he walked around the sanctuary, holding high the Monstrance with the Eucharist, to let Jesus bless his people. He stopped over me, and I started to weep, then more and more as he stood firm, quietly praying, until I was wracked with sobs that resounded throughout the entire sanctuary. Severe though the inner pain was I knew it wasn't going to kill me, but I was fairly certain that the embarrassment would! Still he stood, still I sobbed, and as I stared at the Eucharist, it started to swell, getting bigger and bigger until I was cocooned inside it. It was just Jesus and me. The Lord revealed to me that I was sorrowing for the pain and darkness in so much of the Church and for our lack of power. And he loved me, sweetly, gently. The white marshmallow cloud receded, and I was calm once more, smiling at Fr. Jozo as he smiled back. It was beautiful. As Father knelt at the altar, he cried out, "Thank you, Lord, for hearts that are open."

It made me think of the scripture that says that God's people will not turn to him lest he heal them (Isaiah 6:10). We're afraid of the pain that is already inside us, bursting to be let out, but it's freedom when it does. Releasing the pain was a blessing, but God in his mercy made sure it was public to get a bunch of pride out as well! If we had no priests, we would have no Jesus alive in the Eucharist. The more the priests operate in the supernatural, the more Jesus we get. He comes through their love. That love is Jesus; his love meets us right where we're at, and it goes where the Church can't go, deep into our souls and into our everyday lives.

His love came for my ex-boss, Michael Magee, who had developed lung cancer and was dying, though we didn't know how close it was. He was a Brit and hadn't been in the U.S.A. very long, but long enough to get himself a lovely little wife, Pam, who was a fallen away Catholic. She called me, in great distress at his sickness, and after a while, she let me lead her to the Lord. Awesome! She wanted Mike to have some of the love she felt, but he wasn't playing.

"No thanks," he said, until he found himself getting worse and fear set in.

He called me, and I prayed with him, talked with him, taught him and answered his questions. He was cagey. I discovered, on his bookshelf, a bunch of books on theology and religion that showed me that he had been seeking for a long time. He had just been looking in the wrong place. Reading about the Church will never convert a soul, but how could he have known that? What he needed was a personal relationship with Jesus and Mary and their love for him. He'd never had a real family, and that was what he needed. In my prayers, it became clear that the Lord would have healed him for the ministry, had he come when first asked. Now the cancer had too much of a hold, and the Lord was going to take him home. At least he was going home! I knew it. That put the wind in my wings, and I stepped up my efforts. One day when we were talking, he got it; he simply got the understanding of God's love for him, and the scales fell from his eyes. He surrendered his life into Jesus' hands, and that was so good, except that now he was very ill. He was in and out of hospital until one day Pam called me, from the hospital, and told me he was asking for her rosary. That was my cue to get over there. I visited that Sunday afternoon for a couple of hours and didn't get home until one week later!

When I arrived, I couldn't find Mike. I had checked and double-checked the floor, and the room, when I realized that I had passed him by, twice. I didn't recognize him or the tiny woman bent over the bed with her head in her hands, all alone. "Pam," I asked. She looked up. Bless her little heart, she had already buried one husband, and here she was about to do the same with another with the same filthy disease. My heart tore. I went in and found him so ill that I couldn't leave her with no one to comfort her, and she desperately needed sleep. I was ill myself, but when you're in the Lord, in a deep way, these things are apt not to show to others. So, I stayed, for days. When it was clear that the end would be soon, she and I left the room and went downstairs to discuss what to do with Mike's body when he passed. We were rent with grief, and I didn't have a clue as to how to help her. I'd never seen any-

one die. I'd never been involved with a funeral. Pam couldn't take
it in that because I was in the Church, it didn't follow that I knew
anything of the dead and dying. My ministry was to the living, and
I knew nothing of the other. We talked round and round until we
had to go back upstairs with nothing resolved.

She was numb as a zombie, and I was beside myself. On the
way upstairs, I said, "What we need is a Catholic priest, any
Catholic priest, to tell us what to do."

"Where are we going to find one?" Pam asked, as we stepped
out of the elevator. The floor was deserted except for one figure
walking away from us.

I blurted out, "If that isn't the backside of an old Catholic
priest, then I don't know what is. Father?" I called out.

"Yes, child," was the instant response as he turned around to
look at us. Now wasn't that a beautiful sound to my ears? Talk
about an angel. Oh, joy, I was never so happy to see a priest in all
my life. I ran towards him, crying out as I went, "Father! Please
help us? This is Pam. Her husband's dying, and we haven't a clue
what to do. He's not a member of a church. I've worked with him,
I'm a lay minister, and he received Jesus and Mary. He wanted to
join the Church, but the cancer got him first. What do we do when
he dies? We don't know what to do."

"Where is the boyo?" he asked, with his lovely, gentle, Irish
lilt. We showed him the room and he said, "Sure, and I've already
been in there," peering at the name on the door. "Magee, right
enough," he said. "I've done the lad. There was nobody about, so I
paid a little visit. When I saw the rosary and the scapular, I thought
to myself, "The lad's one of ours", so I gave him the double blessing.

"But, Father," I said, horrified, "he wasn't a Catholic."

"Well, he is now," he chuckled, right pleased with himself!
"The boy's heart's as good as gold," he said, beaming all over his
precious face.

How we rejoiced. We rushed back in to see Mike, gurgling
horribly as he strived for breath and not having spoken a word in
three days.

"Mike," I said, "whether you like or not, you've been blessed by the Church. The Catholics claimed you while we were down-stairs!"

His head lifted a fraction off the pillow and he let rip with an "AMEN!" that soared all the way to heaven. We couldn't believe our ears. What a moment and what a gift. We were so happy. My friend got his beautiful burial, and his wife got a modicum of peace in an agonizing situation. God has his ways of making sure his men are right where he wants them. Only God!

It takes my breath away to think how many events hang by a thread and how much orchestration has to go into each one of them, such as popping that priest right where he was needed. Or was he an angel? To this day Pam says that she heard him but she never saw him. He gave us the name of a priest who would help us arrange the funeral out of town in The Woodlands, and was gone. With that decided, I grabbed the Yellow Pages and started in on funeral homes. What a fraud! Shame on them! It took only three calls to discover that the same items could cost thousands of dollars difference, depending on where you went, but I took the time to do comparisons and got something within reason, given that we were late to do it. When Mike breathed his last, and we were free to leave the hospital, we still had to finalize the funeral arrangements and organize the reception for Pam's guests. This I knew I absolutely could not do, as I was already over the top. Thank God for the body of Christ. I called my dear friend and prayer group leader at Mount Carmel, Georgia-Anne Ethridge. She is your classic Church lady who knows how to get things done, and because of her personal style, they are done well and apparently effortlessly! She took the whole thing off my hands, brilliant as she is at hospitality, which is, admittedly, her super-natural gifting. She rallied the troops who turned out in convoy from Houston to The Woodlands, bearing gifts of smiles, food and hard work. They took all anxiety right out of our hands. Pam was in a fog, and I wasn't much better, but Georgia-Anne stepped into the breach and hosted the occasion to the manner born, with gra-ciousness and warmth. I am so grateful to her and to my sisters in Christ who turned out that day. Only Our Lady full of grace and her children could have organized it so well, with such love and compassion. It's not just priests that Jesus uses to bring supernatural help.

Talking of Mount Carmel reminds me of a Pastor, Fr. Roy Ontiveros, a spirit-filled Carmelite. Jesus used him in yet a different way. The illness that had been insidiously coming upon me finally struck me down, and I was at death's door. I didn't have a doctor, so I was late to be diagnosed. Eighty Megs of Prednisone blew me up like the Michelin man; my hair fell out, and I looked like a bald gargoyle. Not nice! I hadn't been to church for a long time. This feast day, I thought to creep in the side door for Mass. I was slow; it was pouring rain, and I was late. Mass had started. As I opened the door, a gust of wind grabbed hold of it and slammed it shut behind me with a tremendous racket. Wonderful! All I needed was everybody staring at me! An unloving priest would have drawn me a look; a loving one would have ignored me, but this one did neither. Fr. Roy, full of fun, youthful and warm, grinned so broadly and with such unutterable joy at the sight of me that I felt it took all his constraint not to bound down the altar steps to hug me. It was great! I felt like a young thing! I will never forget it. Just when I most needed comfort, God showed up in his priest. What's more, that precious priest has prayed for me daily ever since. You have no idea what a privilege that is, and how rare. His spirit is pure delight. The prayer of a holy man is powerful, and Fr. Roy has truly helped to sustain me through very rough passage. I am grateful, and God will bless him; indeed, I believe he has already.

Mary also has a way of using her priests to get her message across, not that these others aren't hers! Priests revere Mary as a role model of humility and obedience. She used Fr. Stephano Gobbi, a little Italian priest tucked away in his homeland, to move me along. He was minding his own business when the Blessed Virgin Mary called him to cover the earth with the messages she would give him, to be compiled into her book To My Beloved Priests. He started the Marian Movement of Priests, which includes laity, under Mary's leadership, and simply records what she tells him interiorly. Mary, to me, is the prophet of prophets for the end time. Many nights, when in darkness and despair with nowhere to turn, I turned to my Mother, flicked open her book and found a powerful word to gentle my heart or rouse my spirit. The messages are for the whole church, not just Catholics, and why not? Mary isn't Catholic. Neither is her beloved Son! First, they are Jews. Secondly, they want the Gospel spread to all who will listen. We, the original Church, are just especially blessed to have had her from the beginning at the Cross-when Jesus told us to take her as our Mother and again at the birth of the Church at Pentecost. Mary is the Mother of all humans, just as Jesus is Lord of everyone, whether they know it or not. Some like to separate Mary from the Holy Spirit, but as Fr. Francis Frankovich, CC, likes to ask, "When did they get a divorce?" Exactly! Together they brought Jesus to the earth the first time, and together they will do it again the second time, no question!

Fr. Gobbi, unwittingly, brought me a personal message from Our Lady. On one of his visits to Houston, I wandered off from the crowd to pray. I found a room empty but for a statue of Mary, set on a small stage. Her face was tender and sweet and just what I needed to soften the hard place within me, so I stood in front of her, pondering all that I had heard, while praying in the spirit, oblivious to the people who were quietly gathering around. Next thing I knew, Fr. Gobbi was on the stage beside me. It became clear that the purpose of this gathering was for the mothers to hand over their babies to Fr. Gobbi so he could present them to Jesus and Mary. However, the mothers were nearer to me than to him, so they gave them to me to pass to him. Oh, dear God! The little man was weary and not easily amused, and this caper was not well received. He shot me a look every time I handed him a child. Yet, graciously, he let me remain, so there was nothing to do but look holy and beat a hasty retreat as soon as I could. It was a truly awful moment, particularly as my "thing" was not to be noticed! Still, it was too unusual to be allowed to slip by without asking our Mother what she was up to. It was her way of putting the message deeper into my heart that she would be calling me to help her bring souls to Jesus, all for his glory. A holy set up, and not for the first time either! Like Mother, like Son! She used her beloved priest for her purpose, just as Jesus does. See, it runs in the Family!

CHAPTER EIGHT
ROUND AND ROUND THE MULBERRY BUSH

Despite having fun with God's sporadic supernatural interventions, I was growing ever restless in my Catholic faith. I felt so alone. On occasion, our Father would send encouragement from a rare "other," like the prophetic desert voice of a certain Walter Rode, or the constant and faithful love, prayers and tender hospitality of Betty Doyle, servant and minister of Jesus' Living Waters, and her loving husband, Bill. I cannot express enough my thanks to Dr. Alfonso and Cora Cordoba, and to the lovely Katrin. Their longtime friendship, whether or not they understood my "new" lifestyle, and their provision for my material needs, went far beyond any call of kindness, and always came precisely when most needed. Without these "kisses," life would have been almost untenable. My heart will ever be touched by the few who wanted nothing from me but friendship. How rare and beautiful is that, and a true gift from God that is so typical of him. He so wants us loved! Still, and yet, my life in Christ had grown dull. I threw myself into everything previously described hoping that, eventually, it would pay off and bring me life. It didn't, and there seemed nothing left to do or add. There had to be more, but what and where? Fifteen years of my life of "keeping the rule" was enough. My silent scream had become one endless, gnawing ache. I felt old, blah, and finished, and I started to wonder if the practices were, after all, an end, in and of themselves, a dead end at that. Admittedly, they had brought me far, but does it matter how long a journey is or how much extraordinary ground has been covered if it ends against a brick wall? I felt that all of my diligence and dedication should lead somewhere other than to the fulfillment of itself. I was going round and round the religious/spiritual mountain, ever mindful that the only difference between a rut and a grave is the dimension! A spiritual director may have been able to help, but I couldn't find one, just as I couldn't find a helpful confessor.

It kept going back to this. Jesus died to set us free and I felt in chains. He wants us to break out of confinements and to investigate the truth of our lives for ourselves. If we are thrust, too soon, into 'Jesus died so you must serve' we miss the truth that he died for love of us. We think he died for our service. Therein lies the bondage. He died to set us free to take an honest look at our lives and see how we line up with his best for us. Then, when we find the error of our ways and seek him with our whole heart, with our punctured lives held out to him, in tentative trust, it really means something, to us and to him. When it's worked through until that part is perfected Jesus has won a friend, which means the world to him. He doesn't have too many and it's all he really wants. He can't have real fellowship with slaves yet all he heard from me were rattling chains! I had to be free if my life was to mean anything and to mean anything it, ultimately, had to become his. How could I give it to him when I'd already given it over to 'servitude'?

I was bound in fear and 'rules', not just mine but everyone else's too! I didn't think I had the right to leave the parish because we have to grow where we're planted, right? But what if you stop growing because the pot's too small? What then? It's clear to me now but it wasn't then. I hadn't even admitted to myself the depth of what I was feeling and thinking about the turn my life had taken. I was so lost, so hurt inside. Years later, Fr. Sean Wenger said that God's first gift to me was me, my very self. I had a problem with that at first, but, of course, he was right. My Father in Heaven didn't give my life to the Church, he gave it to me, but he couldn't impact it in a right way until I got the revelation that, primarily, the choice was mine as to what I wanted to do with it. Yet, come to think of it, I always knew. When I was a child, my competitive parents would ask, "Whose are you?"

My answer was always the same, "I'm nobody's; I'm my very own."

That little girl got it right. Maybe you don't know, either, that your life belongs to you. It does. No wonder I felt enslaved in a dark world of joyless drudgery; I kept giving myself away without expecting return or reward. That felt holy, it felt like the right thing to do, but was it? How could it be when God says he rewards those who work diligently? When we're open to receive, he loves to pour it out, blessings that we can't even hold, he says! How did we get to be so skewed?

I was jealous of non-denominational Christians who worked for Jesus, who served him together, loving him, sharing him and his ways, who seemed to be free! I knew only how to serve the Church. One pastor said in his homily that some of the most important people in the parish were those who put out the Missalettes. Oh, help me, Jesus! Talk about trying my patience. Not to say that it's not helpful work. Of course, it is. All work is fruitful, but it's hardly life or death. The work of Jesus is, and I was dying on the vine for lack of inspiration and development towards that goal. I hungered for like souls, for kindred spirits, but I wouldn't dare make a move without the Lord's leading, not out of fear, but because it simply doesn't work! There's no happiness outside of his umbrella of grace. I'd been there with bells on, and I was never going there again. I prayed, and I prayed, and, finally, he answered by a circuitous route via California, on a work of mercy for one week to escort an elderly couple on vacation. It was probably one of the most humiliating and painful experiences of my life, compounded by crippling ill health, but the sacrifice brought reward. I was, of course, in telephone contact with Fr. Tom regarding my painful dilemma, and he believed the Lord had a place for me by a body of water. He also gave me a scripture that said that the new thing would cost me everything. It did, indeed, but later with that.

When I returned from California, I was shocked to see that the palm tree in front of my house was struck to the ground and straddled the street. What on earth? The neighbors said there had been no storm, but that the tree had been hit by freak lightening. Then, I knew for sure that I was to pack up and leave. How did I know?

Palms are my favorite trees; they remind me of my Lady Mary, and there was one such in front of the house that I was considering leasing. On looking up, I saw that the branches had rotted with a freeze, but green sprouts were showing through.

I said, "If the tree lives, I stay; if the tree dies, I go."

It had flourished, and now it was dead, felled to the ground by the hand of God. I stood in my study, leaning on my desk, still in my overcoat, and pondered where to go. The scripture Father gave me popped into my head, "You do not have far to go." The nearest thing to me was the desk drawer. I opened it, and, lo and behold, there was literature tucked in there from the Community of Jesus at Cape Cod. I guess the Atlantic is as big a body of water as one would need for confirmation! I had been in touch with that community some months before but rejected a visit, for they seemed too 'Catholic', even although they were Episcopalian. They were supposed to be a sister community to Redeemer, which would have been awesome, but they weren't really. Nevertheless, true to the prompt, I contacted them again, and they told me I would have to fly up there to see if they would accept me. That was a hugely expensive trip. I arrived in time for what seemed like the coldest Christmas in history! I froze, inside and out. They were not the friendliest people in the world at that time of year, but I didn't care. It was where Jesus wanted me, and that was all I needed to know. I was told to pack my car, including computer, and to expect to be there for some time. I flew back to Houston to finish dismantling a home and a ministry. I opened the door of the house and let people come in to help themselves to whatever was there. What was left, I gave away or put in the attic of a past member of the old prayer group. She was a poor soul, so I furnished a large studio bedroom in her house with my bedroom furniture, desk, couch, chairs, and accessories, so she could rent it out and assist with household expenses. That done, I was about ready for departure when my good friend Helen entered in. It was January 1996 when I was set to go, not the best weather to be heading northeast from Texas, and she was not impressed.

"I'm coming with you," she announced.

"Incredibly kind," I said, "but, no, thank you. I've no room for you in this little Honda, besides which it's stuffed to the gills."

"Empty something out," she insisted, "I'm coming with you."

I was also concerned about her back injury, acquired from a bout of madness when, in her salad days, jumping out of airplanes passed for being fun! Mad dogs and Englishmen, I tell you! I continued to argue when she clinched it.

"Liz" she said, 'You're being absolutely ridiculous. You haven't driven further north than 1960, for God's sake, and I'm coming with you."

And that was that, and she was right. F.M.1960, for your information, is the loop that runs around Houston! God bless her for that and much else, for that's how she is with all her friends. That's just Helen. She was squashed into that sardine can of a car in pained misery until she ducked out at Washington D.C., in order to get back to her very busy desk. She took vacation time to come with me, and, believe me, that cross-country drive was an adventure of the best and worst kind, fraught with complexity. I call the love my friends have for me pretty radical, don't you?

Two hilarious moments spring to mind from that drive. The first was in Louisiana, which, as you know, has a reputation for exceptionally good food. We love to eat! It was quite dark when we saw a seriously weathered sign, suggestive of an establishment of considerable duration. Excellent! We shot off the main thoroughfare and motored down a winding dirt road. Our headlamps flickered on thick undergrowth fringing the track as it narrowed ahead of us. Slowly we pulled up to the edge of a swamp, and in the pale, watery moonlight, we saw a long, low, shuttered structure straight in front of us. It lurked on the far side of a ropey wooden bridge, which had seen better days. In for a penny, in for a pound, we agreed to give it a try. The murky mist rising from the swamp was swirling restlessly around us as we gingerly crossed the bridge onto the broken-down verandah and tapped on the door. There wasn't a sound, not a crack of light. The half door opened, and a tall, lean figure slithered silently from behind it as it swiftly closed behind him. His eyes were huge, round, and surely nearly popped clean out of his head at the sight of us. God knows what he expected to find, but it sure as heck wasn't two hungry Brit dames hunting down a gourmet meal! Finally, we got it. This was no restaurant. We told him, overly brightly, why we were here, about the sign on the road, obviously our mistake, and then we started backing off. His eyes didn't flicker even for a second. He just stood and stared. The scene was eerie, but he was alarming. I remember babbling phrases like "wrong turn. . food. .mistake. .so sorry. ." and hearing us become "frightfully" British and polite; with our falsetto tones piercing the oppressive stillness, we stumbled backwards away from what felt like our sure demise! Where were our heads, you might wonder? No idea. I'd been in so many weird places that this could have been just one more "atmospheric" night out. I'd also been around enough to recognize that we had stumbled upon things that were not for us to know, things of the dark side. On the other hand, who knows? Maybe we put the fear of God into them, whatever they were up to! Wouldn't it be hilarious if they thought we strange creatures were a visitation from the Light! In any event, it was one chilling escapade that we could probably have done without!

To do God's work, I had been living on my early retirement funds, the end of which would see me cleaned out. Before the journey, I needed to have my eight-year-old Honda Accord serviced. Old Joe Palermo really wanted to help me out, so he took me to his garage and introduced me, hoping to get me a good price. Ostensibly, I was leaving Houston for good, so this garage man of good repute saw his chance and would not release the car until I paid him $2000, including, how could I forget, $49 for windscreen wipers and $30 for a gas cap. You get the picture. I was furious, and I was hurt for old Joe who took it upon himself to be ashamed that I was shafted. I comforted myself that, at least, the car would last for many years, so we set off with peace of mind in that regard. Now, somewhere in this great and mighty land, we pulled over for a burger, since there's nothing else out there, and happy we were to have it. When we got out of the car, I noticed a stream of rainbow colored oil running away from the engine. I exploded with fear and anger!

"I don't believe it," I screeched. "After what I paid that horrible man, I now have a leak?" I was livid. "All that money that I don't have?"

Helen shouted back at me, "For heaven's sake, will you shut up about the money and PRAY!"

I turned on her and shouted back, "You pray!"

She yelled back, "You're the bloody pro!"

I was silenced, completely. Then I roared with laughter. It was the funniest thing I'd ever heard, a lay person being called a "prayer pro." It tickled my funny bone and took me by surprise, not only because I didn't know that she was a praying person, but also because I never thought of her as thinking of me like that. I didn't talk much of my call at that time, or so I thought. Anyway, as God would have it, there was a mechanic alongside the eatery. I drove very carefully over there, a nervous wreck, and told him my tale of woe. I left the car with him while we ate. When we went back, my heart was in my mouth, worried that I couldn't pay for it. He looked at me, shaking his head and rolling his eyes, and said, slowly in a flat tone, "Ma'am, there's nothing wrong with the car. It's water from the air conditioner."

Darn. He had to be thinking I was a moron! I certainly did the credibility of women no good that day. I'd made all that fuss about nothing! Ah, well. Thank you, Jesus, what's to say! I was chagrined in more ways than one, but thanks to Helen for going above and beyond and putting up with it all!

I arrived at my new Community just in time to endure severe snow, ice and Lent. Wonderful! I was given my quarters and a list of house rules. I lived and worked in one place and slept in another, a few snowy fields away. Every time I think of the place, even all these years later, I have the same scene in my head. A bell was rung for prayer five times a day, prayer in Latin chant yet, as part of their Lenten practice. Everybody dropped what they were doing and headed for the church. They removed mufflers, boots and greatcoats and donned religious robes to enter the sanctuary, only to reverse the entire process half an hour later. Phew! That's hard on the able bodied, never mind the half crock that I was. I was truly exhausted when I arrived and was never able to catch up. I'd been religiously broken in by two other communities, so a third time proved to be particularly tedious. Trudging to the church and back was such a pain, but it's all about discipline and sacrifice. I felt I showed extraordinary restraint in not killing somebody! Now, that's discipline! The heavily "religious" aspect of parish life that got to me in Houston was beginning to look attractive. I thought getting away from Catholicism would be a breath of fresh air, but, instead, I felt like I'd fallen into a time warp.

"Why do you all wear robes and chant in Latin?" I asked.

"Our leaders believe we need to return to our roots," was the reply.

The Catholic Church had just got out of all of that, and here I was, jumping from the frying pan into the burny, burny fire, more "Catholic" than the Catholics! Oh, help! I had no clue that there are many legalistic denominations within the body of Christ, not just us. What on earth was God up to with me? This community was formal in every way with "excellence" being their motto. They were sincere, no question, and the teaching tapes I bought were right on, but everyone seemed a trifle uptight for my taste. There wasn't a lot of laughter. However, I am grateful for the experience. I learned much and I was healed much, especially on my child-hood. It's the same Atlantic Ocean as I grew up with in Scotland, same salty, brisk air, same seaweed stench and the same seagulls, I'm sure. Tears would pour down my face as I walked the dog along the coastland that tore at my heart. Most of all, their stringent ways propelled me and healed me of the grief I had harbored over the loss of relationship with my daughter, my only child and my primary reason for living for so many years.

No experience is lost on us. This was no exception, but my material wealth was. One paid a high dollar cost for the privilege of serving there. I was virtually penniless when I left, but richer in other ways. What else did I learn? I had always been obedient, but did I always have the best attitude? I was cured of that over there. I was crying out to Our Lady to help me to sustain despite the physical exhaustion. She dropped joy on me, the joy of service. What a gift to stand me in good stead for the rest of my life! Whatever I was asked to do, it was a pleasure to do it, although some doubted my sincerity, I know. Who could blame them? I wasn't supposed to be having a good time! It's so easy to judge others by ourselves, isn't it? The scripture Fr. Tom gave me proved correct and right on the button: (Ecclesiasticus 51:23-30). It was no cakewalk and very humbling, but I was much the better for it. Isn't it just like Jesus to send you to a place worse than the one you left to make you settle down where he wants you? Uh huh! I thought I would be there a year, or permanently, depending upon how it worked out. It was only six or seven weeks when Our Lady unexpectedly called me back to Houston the very night before they asked me to leave. They said they had "nothing to teach me there!" That sounded like a crock, but with God, who knows. They were amazed when I said I already knew I was to leave. In that short time, I had suffered much and had therefore changed much, which is the whole point. Belle was the most fascinating person I encountered there. I really liked her, and if we'd met elsewhere, I think we could have been good friends. There's always heaven! The ride back through snow and ice and driving wind, with my little Honda bouncing like a cork over the Blue Ridge Mountains, ensured my delight in returning to sunny Houston and a fresh start, yet again. Mount Carmel to Redeemer to Mount Carmel to Cape Cod to Mount Carmel, three times around the mountain.

The room I had furnished for someone else became my room. Joyce had not yet rented it out. She was the only person to write to me, saying how much she missed me and that the room was mine if I returned. What a God! I returned to Mount Carmel to worship quietly and to keep a low profile and to do it all midst the luxury of my very own belongings.

After several months, the Lord told me to worship at the Catholic Charismatic Center, full-time, and not spasmodically as I had done over the years. Shortly after that, still in 1997, I was struck down with illness and was virtually bed-ridden for about two years and housebound for many more than that. The Holy Spirit taught me much in that time, and my spiritual life took a completely different turn, though always within the boundaries of Church teaching. My belief that the Catholic Church is the true church is solid, but further overhaul wouldn't do some of it any harm, it seems to me! Doesn't Jesus say he wants us to be filled with the Holy Spirit, to heal the sick, drive out demons and raise the dead? Of course, he does. Doesn't he say he wants us to meet together every day for church and fellowship and family: to eat, laugh, learn, teach, dance, rejoice, and to help and love one another in a way unique only to Christians? He does. So what's there to argue about? You could say that he wanted that in the past, but not now. How come? Is he alive? Then why would he change his mind regarding the teachings that cost him his life and the lives of many others whom he cherished? His people were different, granted, and they were known to be. These early Christians lived life to the fullest and had a very good time doing it despite persecution! They had such joy! How I wanted to find people like that? Where were they, I wondered? I wanted them so much it hurt! (Acts 2:42-47)

I attended the Center, but I still wasn't finding what I was seeking. It was close, but still not the vision. I prayed and prayed some more in my continued restlessness. Then I heard of a community in Denver, Colorado, called The Beatitudes. They were small, but they sounded like my kind of people. My contact with them, including the priests, perhaps particularly the priests, was loving, sweet and welcoming. Despite the fact that I was in a wheelchair, they were happy to receive me. How rare is that! They are Catholic, enjoy Hebrew dancing, and priests and laity live in community together. How lovely! I believed Jesus was giving me the desire of my heart and that it was his idea to send me there. I packed up the house and was set to go when in January 2003 Our Lady said, "It was a test, Elizabeth."

I knew she meant a test of obedience, ever preparing me for the next assignment. She said she would prefer me to stay at the Charismatic Center, but, of course, as always, the choice was mine. So here I am. Pope John Paul II told Archbishop Fiorenza of Galveston-Houston Diocese that "Houston is the city of the future of America." That helped to hold me, always living on a wing and a promise, that's me!

A Maryknoll priest, Fr. Richard Paulissen, founded the Charismatic Center some thirty years ago, and, prior to his retirement, he turned it into a 2400 seat Oratory. He passed the baton to a new order of priests out of Canada. They teach everything that Fr. Tom grounded me in, so I was very excited when I heard that the Companions of the Cross were taking over. Their mission is Evangelization! They are a new Society, raised up by the Holy Spirit for the end time—right up my street! Their "Four Pillars" are Magisterium, Mary, Holy Spirit and the Eucharist. Couldn't be better. That's my call! Thank you, God. Their main thrust is to renew Parish life, which is a hard call. They need our prayers, but they are already showing success. Their call to take over the Center is unique to that place, which is in itself unique. They have an extraordinary role there to support the renewal of the parishes in the Archdiocese and elsewhere. Also, and it is critical, they work to fulfill the call of the Holy Spirit to train up disciples and apostles in the ways of Jesus. It is a privilege to share in this work, with priests who are solid in their call to listen to the Holy Spirit and let him lead. The Center is not church as usual and must never become so! It presents an unparalleled opportunity to serve Jesus and Mary, in many and varied ministries as it establishes itself and prepares for the major thrust. The time is coming when many will be frantic to find help for their souls. I pray we have an army to assist them.

If anyone out there were looking for a venue to bring gifts and talents, to work for the truth, to help us nail down authentic Catholic Christianity, the Center would be a great place to consider. When we give Jesus total control over our lives, everything changes. How much more when we hand over an entire ministry, as Fr. Francis Frankovich, CC, did on Christmas Vigil, 2002, when he dedicated the Center into the hands of the Virgin Mary. Now she is the official head of the household, she will continue to shake us up and move us about until everything is to her satisfaction for the return of her beloved Son. She will not rest until she has the Church on course to heal and restore all people by bringing them to Jesus, all for God's glory. She loves the whole of humanity with unparalleled mercy and compassion.

The Companions come with a love for the unmitigated Gospel. I love that! Since I've invited you to come, let me introduce you to some of them. Take Father Dan Cross at Mass one day in the past. He is no longer in Houston. He stood before us repentant. With strong voice, he asked our pardon for treating us with less love than he felt he should. He went on to talk about all the times we had been hurt by priests in a variety of ways and begged our pardon on behalf of the entire priesthood, hoping to bring us to reconciliation and forgiveness. I choked up. He was talking to my heart. I'd been so hurt by priests that I could write a whole book on just that, but for what? Priests are a different breed. They just are. They're Jesus' men, and we need to accept them and love them as the unique individuals they are, just as we expect them to do for us. If they break the law, let the law deal with them. Let's not judge them, for judging anyone breaks the law of love to which we are called, and then we're in trouble. It's a life exercise, learning not to judge others, for only God knows the whole story. Let's be merciful to ourselves and forgive. Fr. Dan's sincerity touched me, so I overcame any misgivings and reached out to him after Mass. Despite the restrictions of my wheelchair, he saw me and came to me, seeing that I had a real need. I whispered that I had a quick confession to make. Immediately, he crouched on the floor beside me as I told him how hurt I'd been by priests; although I'd forgiven them, I couldn't get the pain out of my heart. He laid his hands on me, looked in my eyes with beautiful compassion, and stood in for his brothers. He asked forgiveness for all priests for whatever I felt they had done to hurt me so much. Supernatural grace covered me, and the pain was gone, never to return. Glorious relief! That was wonderful, but much better even than that was that I caught his compassion and filled with love and understanding for them instead. I was free! Only Jesus could have done that. I really believe that most priests do the best they know to do, or can do, given their own personal makeup. No one can do better than their best, even if their best is lousy, now can they? In addition, how easy do you think we are to deal with, even the best of us? We are so many to their few.

Father Michael Scherrey, Director and Pastor of the Center, is a giant of a man, doubtless a legacy from his star football days, with a heart as tender as a lamb. How that ties in with having been an unusually successful stockbroker, I've no idea, but that knowledge bodes well to keep our finances straight! Fr. Michael's late entry into the priesthood has been exceptional. His was the first ordination at the Center performed by our new Bishop, who in the space of some three years rose to Archbishop and is now Cardinal Daniel DiNardo. We are so thrilled that God sent the Cardinal here and honored him with a truly beautiful new Co-Cathedral that has really put us, to our pride and joy, on the Houston map. Fr. Michael's ordination was magical, if you will excuse the word and use it in the sense intended. Everyone should be obliged to attend an Ordination: it will fill you with such pride in Jesus and his Church. Cardinal DiNardo is himself a phenomenon, another priest with a difference who has been raised high in his young years. He shines very bright! The Cardinal brings a down-to-earth personality, sincerity and a depth of love that reduced many of us to tears that awesome day. Everything points to something spiritually extraordinary coming out of Houston, just as has been achieved in medicine and space. Consider that the first word from outer space to earth was "Houston." What's that all about? Yay! God calling!

What's more, that very day of his ordination, Fr. Michael was pronounced not only priest but also Director of the Center. How rare to be given a job as well as the office on the same day! What on earth is Jesus up to in that place! It's no wonder it was magical, as that's something else Fr. Michael has up his sleeve. Magic tricks! And they're good, very good. A sign of a misspent youth, I don't wonder. It's something to watch his big old hands perform to get our attention. He is a true pastor; that's his calling. He is a shepherd who ministers with a gentle spirit and truthfulness; he delivers correction with the warmth of a fireside chat. He's also a prayer warrior. When the London trains were bombed, I was distraught over my daughter. I knew she was safe and nowhere near the havoc, but it brought home to me how much I miss her. Broken relationships are hell, aren't they?

Life is so short and unpredictable and I was inconsolable. I had the prayer team pray with me, to no avail. I cried my way through Mass; couldn't stop. I had more people pray for me. I still couldn't stop. As I was leaving, I saw Fr. Michael. He laid his hands on my head; in a couple of sentences, the crying had stopped, and the pain was gone. Awesome! Healing priests, that's what we need. Fr. Michael says he's just a "good ole boy" from Arkansas, but don't you believe it. He's sharp as a tack, and he'll jump all over you if you cross him on The Church! He is Magisterium nailed down! "Yes," he'll say, "I hear you, but The Church says.................." That's the end of that! I guess he's the "Magisterium" of the four pillars. That's Fr. Michael, and he's very dear to me.

Father Sean Wenger is now Pastor of Our Lady of Mount Carmel Parish, my old stomping ground. Interesting, huh. He was one of the original Companions at the Center. For me, he represented the pillar of the "Eucharist." He's Canadian, so if you think of winter athleticism caged up in 100-degree heat in Houston, Texas, you pretty much have Fr. Sean. He enjoys being a priest, is passionate about furthering the Kingdom, is highly intellectual and has challenged my thinking on many things, not least myself. That was fun; I loved that! However, his greatest gift to me was himself in the Eucharist. Before we went up to receive, Fr. Sean made a stand from his gut, and I heard it! Strutting up and down like a caged lion, he proclaimed, so crisply and distinctly that you could hear a pin drop in that huge Sanctuary, "If you do not believe, do not receive!" Then, "If you are not in good standing with the Catholic Church, do not receive!"

I was deeply convicted that it is a tremendous privilege to be one with Christ in his living, supernatural flesh and blood, and that I qualified! I qualified! I was electrified. Finally, I belonged. My misgivings at being a newcomer melted away. It had taken only twenty years! The Church had received me. That's how I felt!

Father Ed Wade is our "Holy Spirit" pillar, our Evangelist! He's an ex-Marine and still loves taking that hill! He's our street preacher or would be if he could get the chance. He's on fire with the Holy Spirit and puts it out there, clearly, just what will become of us if we don't fly straight. He has a heart of gold that he works hard at hiding, and he's a man after my own heart when it comes to being a straight arrow. At the same time, he is a man of deep prayer, and I have seen him melt in the face of another's pain, gathering them up in his arms as a true Father. That is so beautiful to see, how he longs to heal God's people, and does, especially lately through Theophostic prayer. He takes enormous pleasure in reminding us, at every possible opportunity, that we all deserve to burn in hell, he the foremost, were it not for Jesus! He's a rich, salty character and delightful if you've the stomach for the truth. I love it, and him, very much! Now, he's really embarrassed!

One Thursday night Fr. Ed was celebrating the Healing Mass. Three days earlier, I had been told that I would never walk again and was signed out on permanent disability. I kept it to myself. Fr. Ed was preaching on Peter walking on water and challenged us to do likewise, to have faith that God would heal us. He was at the altar, looming large and with a sideways glance at me, said, "Take a step of faith and walk."

What? You've got to be kidding, Father! I was hearing nothing from the Lord. Nothing. Once again, this time with eyes straight ahead, he barked, "Take a step of faith and walk!"

He was beginning to look uncomfortable, and, honestly, I felt for him stuck up there all by himself. Did he know something I didn't know, I wondered. Training kicked in to obey the priest, so, noblesse oblige; I made a gesture, a feeble attempt to get out of the wheelchair. As I did so, people ran forward to help me. I was now as embarrassed as he was. Suddenly, before I knew it, I was out of the chair and walking swiftly up and down in front of the altar. I remember asking someone, "Am I walking?"

"Yes," she said, "perfectly".

I knew I was moving, but it felt like it had nothing to do with my limbs or me. I wasn't floating, just moving without myself. I guess Father Ed did know something I didn't know after all, or else he stepped out in faith himself! Either way, whatever it was, God honored it. Rose, the Deacon's wife, who is no youngster, was one of those who came to my aid. She has a hysterical tale to tell about it. As she put her hand under my arm, she thought, "Lord! This woman weighs a ton. She'll never get out of this chair." Then, right behind it, "Oh no, I'm a Deacon's wife. I'm not supposed to think like that. Sorry, Lord, you can do anything you want." I became light as a feather! So funny! God's ways are His and His alone. That was four years ago, and I'm still wobbling around. This year, 2008, my doctor took me aside to tell me that, sick as I was, she expected by now that I would be on 20 medications a day, including morphine, and totally bedridden. Not so, all thanks to Jesus and Fr. Ed. That could have been my future did they not have me out of that chair and on to a slow journey to recover muscle strength. I'm walking, not perfectly and only in short bursts, but I'm walking. And it will get better yet! God is doing a total healing, and he will not stop a work he has begun, now will he, especially now that I've told the world!

Fr. Francis Frankovich is our elder statesman. He has a deep love for Mary and the Holy Spirit. He was raised in California and loves the Hispanic people in a special way. He speaks the language fluently, which I'd love to be able to do if it dropped on me in the night! All of these gifts make him extremely valuable to the Center where we have a large community of Hispanics, red hot for Our Lord and Lady in their love and praise of them. The Holy Spirit uses Fr. Francis in outstandingly spiritual ways through his homilies, especially when he is preaching his love for the Virgin Mary. I have had several remarkable, personal, supernatural experiences at his Masses.

As a result, I am absolutely convinced that not much is going to happen these days in Catholic arenas that do not heartily embrace Mary. She is the powerful, interceding Mother of Jesus. She is the well-beloved Spouse of the Holy Spirit, bearing and distributing his gifts. She is our Mother who nurtures, teaches, and kisses us better! More than that, she is the woman whose heel will crush the serpent's head right out of our lives and out of the world! That's one woman worth hanging in with, people. Mary is never far from her Son, and the Holy Spirit is never far from her. We desperately need the prophetic to stir up our apathy; Mary and the Holy Spirit are just the two to do it with signs and wonders, bringing Jesus again to the forefront of our hearts and minds. Only when we really grasp what it means to be a blood-bought Christian and what we have been saved from, will we rise up with fervor to reach out to others to save them from the fate worse than death: it is, you know, far, far worse.

It is hard for people raised in religion to believe that they need saving, just as people in the world system need saving. This is especially true of Catholics who are privileged to receive the very life's blood of Christ into them, and, therefore, erroneously believe that they will have eternal life based on that alone. It is truly understandable that they would think so, but even the grace of the Eucharist is conditional on our growing in love for others, for God, and for ourselves by getting rid of personal sin. That is the one command that must be taken seriously, the command to love. Religious pursuits are empty if they do not lead us to love. The Eucharist is to help us to do that, so, really, we have less excuse than others to stay blind. Let's give Jesus a real treat by becoming excited about him. He wants happy, loving people around him, enjoying him, talking with him and loving being together. That's the true Church, the one that Jesus left. With a zealous priesthood and a zealous laity, not only on the same page but standing on the same Word, there will be no stopping us!

And there are different avenues to expressing that Word. Have you ever visited heaven on earth? I have! I'm talking of a Charismatic Holy Mass! It's magnificent, people, when you're in the presence of the Holy Spirit. Come with me! The Sanctuary is filled with all of our beautiful Guardian Angels, the Angels of the altar, and those of the priests. Can you imagine how many there are when Jesus shows up? Together with them, we are singing God's praises, especially with musicians following the ebb and flow of the Holy Spirit. The Word is not read, but proclaimed! The priest speaks to us, God's heart to ours, revealing the power and revelation of the Scripture just proclaimed through the Holy Spirit. The priests offer us up, incense making us a sweet fragrance to the Lord, cleansed by Jesus' bloody sacrifice as he makes himself present to us. Oh, glory! The praises rise, louder and louder, sweeter and sweeter, as priests and congregation, angels and saints above and in our midst, one body, burst into spontaneous song and worship in heavenly tongues. Oh, my, there's no sound on earth like that. Then, our magnificent royal Lord Jesus says, come, beloved! Eat! Drink! How could that not be heavenly? There's no song sweet enough or rich enough to express the glory of Jesus alive and well in his Church. So far, it doesn't happen often when everything in the Mass is totally united with the Holy Spirit, but when it does there's nothing like it.

It is now apparent that what I was seeking, am seeking, is this Kingdom of God, which has not yet come! Bummer! But, at least,

I have satisfied myself that what I long for does not yet exist here. No wonder I was having a problem. So, what to do? The only thing left to do is to settle at the next best place, which, for me, is the Catholic Charismatic Center where God sent me. My, my, he really knows his kids! Everything I have shared with you points to God having plans for the place, that's obvious. I am almost bursting with anticipation for what he has decreed for Houston, and my trips around the mulberry bush have, mercifully, occupied me until he does. It's going to happen. I don't know what it is, but it is going to happen! Mercy and compassion will flow in this city. We must be ready. He will use us to bring his Kingdom, people, but to use us, he must prepare us. Open up and let him in, wherever you are. That's what it's all about, brothers and sisters. For now!

CHAPTER NINE
THE MOST RADICAL LOVE OF ALL

What's it all about? Some years ago, Helen, my friend, asked me that. She meant, why are we here at all? Why are we on the earth? I'm sure she had her own slant; she just wanted to hear mine. I hadn't sufficiently evolved to give a satisfactory answer. There was so much to say that I didn't know what to say. I gave her the stock response of love God, self and neighbor, which was true enough, but it was bare bones, without flesh. If it needed flesh, it needed Jesus. So, here it is, here's what it's become all about for me. It's not so much that we love Jesus, but that he first loved us. I know we know that, but do we get it that the beginning and end of everything starts right there? We're here to know how much God loves us! We're here to want that love, to reach out and grab onto it, to believe it, rejoice in it and roll around in it to our heart's content. When we get that, we've made it. We're safe. That's it. He'll do the rest.

For some, it's easy, I daresay. For me, it's been a lifetime, but it's key. He wants so much for us to feel his love, his affection. Did I say feel it? Yes, I did! I know! I know! We've been taught not to talk of feelings, but think about it. Without feelings, we're no longer human. Isn't it our job to be fully human? Didn't Jesus wear all his feelings on his sleeve? Is he not our role model? Then if he did, we must. I'm not talking about slinging around a bunch of emotions. Of course not. However, we do need to be in touch with what we feel. When we are, we'll meet God right in there. He doesn't need a load of facts about our lives; he knows those. He wants to know how we feel about what's going on. He wants us to pay a visit and to sit up close with him so that we can feel safe, happy, loved and heard. How else can he know how to help us?

When I was doing inner healing work, it is clear that not all the slapping around we take in this world has prepared us for love. We don't trust it. We don't believe in it. Not only have we not been loved, in many cases, we have been purposefully unloved. Jesus hates our pain and suffering, and he knows that much of it rests in how we feel about things, how we perceive things. I used to preach that he wasn't Dr. Feelgood but that he was Dr. Getbetter. That's idiotic. Sometimes, we can't be made better. But if we can be made to feel better about it, then we can be much happier. Of course, he wants us to feel better, and he can heal our feelings when we tell him about them. He's human, too. Remember? Moreover, he's so sweet in his listening that he really listens, to every word and nuance, no matter how ugly. He wants you well. He didn't strike me off the face of the earth when I fessed up about wanting to kill someone as I tromped through the Cape Cod snow dragging a laundry bag in the middle of the night, now did he? And I didn't care who it was, anyone would do! Did I want to do it? Of course not, but did it feel good to feel it? Absolutely!

We must admit our feelings, at least to ourselves, whether or not it's "nice!" Have you heard of Dr. Ed Smith? As a minister and therapist, he was frustrated about how long it took to heal hurting people and how little time we had left to do it. The Holy Spirit graced him with a revelationary insight for a "feeling" methodology. I have trained in this method, and it's marvelous! It cuts through talk and gets right to feelings, yes, feelings, that are, often as not, hurt by our believing some lie or other! The Holy Spirit roots out the lie, the deception, and sets that precious captive free. That's Theophostic Ministry. On first sight, it's not too different from inner healing, which God also gave us, but he's moving things along for the last days. We are living in a time of extraordinary grace and favor. Why so? God wants as many people free and happy in Jesus before the terrible day of the Lord comes upon us like a thief in the night. I believe we are being primed for the most powerful outpouring of love the world has ever seen since the First Coming and Pentecost.

It will be the precursor to the Kingdom of Love because that is exactly what the new heaven and the new earth will be. The King and Queen of Love are gearing up for our Father's Kingdom to come. That may sound strange to the American democratic ear, but those in Monarchies around the world will have considerably less trouble with it. God is King! Why else would he speak of his Kingdom? Fairy Tales may not be as far-fetched as we'd like to think. No mere human could invent a tale more wondrous, more beautiful, more awesome, more exciting or more adventurous than what God has designed for us in his heavenly Kingdom on earth. How he longs for us to be one with him in one big, happy family, literally, from one end of the earth to the other! He wants to be in the middle of us, romping around, joshing with one another, enjoying one another, telling the stories of the day. He wants intimacy and closeness in his family. He would do away with our absurd, huffy "no talk" rules, with their coldness, distance, rigidity, finger wagging and stubbornness. He hates the standoffish silence that regulates some families. He hates the pain it causes. He hates the tit for tat and the ratatatat that takes so much effort to sustain. How would Jesus like us to deal with our inevitable fallings-out? Easy. You hug, and you love, and you kiss your way through it. You must never, never withhold love for effect, or to gain your own end. Not ever! You can scream and shout, and jump all about, but you must, must love, hold, and kiss while you're saying how mad you are, it will get you to the 'sorry' quicker! Isn't that novel? Trust Jesus to come up with that one! Our love and affection must stand, no matter what, to avoid bitterness and resentment.

He wants us held while in our pain, even if we caused it, indeed, the more so if we caused it. It doesn't matter who started it; both hurt. People are just people to God. All hurt, all need love, and he delights in giving it when he's asked. He holds us through our differences and brings wisdom to make well the wounds. That's love! He wants us to be like that, to be as he is. The big, old, angry God in the sky exists, certainly, but that fury is strictly held in reserve for evil. Our Father loves us, every last one of us, in and out of the Church, every race, creed and nation. Why do

93

you suppose he created us thus in the first place? The three persons in one were not satisfied with just themselves, with just each other. They wanted to love more. They are love, and love must share or pine! God didn't have to pine; he just needed a plan. He started with angels, those beautiful and wondrous creatures! They were not enough. They let him down. Lucifer and his grumbling rebels were thrust out of heaven by the great St. Michael and hurled down to earth. So, God came up with his master plan. Us! He created us! Brilliant! He would make wonderful, individual, entertaining little bundles of love and call them humans. He would pour his love into us, and we would reciprocate with warm intimacy, conversation, fun, laughter and holy kisses. Lovely! A perfect plan.

People long for babies in exactly the same way and for exactly the same reason, as an extension of the love they have for one another. And doesn't that love grow into pride as the babies become adult and start doing really interesting things with their lives? It's the same with God. We're his little babies to delight in, and as we grow, he takes an interest in everything we do, encouraging us to stretch, meet our potential and live fulfilled lives, just like every other doting parent. That's our Dad! That's who he is! He loves! He loves us extravagantly, radically.

How do I know? If I didn't know it personally, and I do, I would only have to look at the great and mighty love that inspired Jesus to do what he did. Let's face it: how do we get our children to do our will? For the most part, we scare them, don't we? Like it or not, we do. How does the Church get us to toe the line? Fear, without question. Ask any normal, garden Catholic what they're mostly afraid of in their faith, and they'll say, "Not getting it right." When you ask what the "it" is, you will draw a blank. They don't know, bless 'em. They're just trying not to offend, trying not to make waves, trying not to draw attention to themselves, trying not to fail or fall. The more fear we are raised in, the more fear we have in life in general, keeping us in line. Jesus' Mother raised him in love so he personified love by his very being, even although he had much to fear. Here's my point: no amount of fear in the world could have put Jesus on that Cross. Only the power of deep, authentic, reciprocal love could have inspired such heroic action. Only a Father's bottomless love for his Son could inspire that Son to leave home, take on another persona, live in exile amongst strangers and finish the way he did and all to please that Father. Think about everything Jesus put himself through to alleviate the pain of the Father he adored. The love between them is immeasurable; it's the most radical love of all, and they yearn to share it with us. When we recognize Christ in each other, on our glowing, joyful faces, we know that we are sharing in that love. The Father and the Son each want to see the other when they look at us. That's what makes us authentic family: Christ in us! We look like each other!

That's what the Trinity wanted. However, it's not what they got. Satan made sure of that. From the Garden, everything went wrong. However, God is in the business of winning us back, one by one, starting with that most radical statement of love in human history: the Cross. Jesus resolved to get us back, but at what anguished cost for both Father and Son! To say nothing of the Mother! Do they suffer still, do you suppose? I used to think that Jesus was all-comfy in heaven, sipping a gin tonic, one leg slung over a chair, job done. Now, I look at us all and the state we are in. Then I have to wonder. In his shoes, would I be satisfied that shedding my blood to jump-start the world into new life would reap such little reward? Had I been Jesus, I would have expected people to be elated to discover that life goes on after death. Look at all the holy people who rose out of their tombs when he gave up his spirit, and many saw them (Matt 27:52-53). The resurrection of so many from the dead proved that it was for us, too, and not just for Jesus. Surely, I'd be thinking, they will choose my Father's way over Satan's eternal darkness. He must be saddened beyond bearing to see how few seek his way and how many will be lost. It's heart breaking.

However, he never quits trying to find people to work through, to bless us, to beckon us. I believe that when people go out of their way for us, it is God's radical love. Be grateful! I've had people approach me with, "You're a Christian, and you have to help me. You have to give me what I want." Really? And what about what I want, like clocking them one on top of the head! Not that I would, but it's a great thought. If they think we have everything, why don't they come and get it for themselves, eh? Because there's a cost they're not prepared to pay. So often, they're ungrateful for what they do have. We can sweat, beg, plead, cry and moan to get what we want. Believe me, I was a pro at all of them and all I got was a bad dose of pride and self-pity as a reward! A better way is to let God know what you need, praise him and thank him, even if it kills you. Rejoice in what you have, and await a happy outcome. That works! Gratitude, when you feel abandoned, is an attitude of radical love.

There are only two great powers in the world, you know, and you are neither of them. There is God and his power of radical love, and there is Satan with his power of fear and hatred. When earthly life is over, we will be with one or the other, up or down. I used to think there was a no man's land. There is not. If there were, who would want to be in it, a place where there's no one? We talk such nonsense out there. And you can't disappear into the big sleep as though you never existed. I thought that, too. Since Jesus went to the Cross to save you from death, you cannot escape eternity. You will live forever in one place or the other, heaven or hell. One is pure joy and the other unmitigated torment. And it's forever, people. We cannot fathom it in it's horror but it is the truth: it's the place for rebels. That's why we must choose for God and we must choose here. It's too late once you've closed your eyes. You will open them on the other side in exactly the same spiritual condition as when you closed them. It's just a blink, people, between heaven and hell! If you think you are a free agent here, you are deceived. You belong to Satan, by default, until you give yourself to Christ. Don't fall for the lie that you are your own man. To be free of God's ways here is to be free of God's ways there. That's hell. People take their own lives in order to escape the pain and misery that they will take with them. Oh, no! What a waste, what a tragedy. This is where we work it all out, right here. If we start here and don't get finished, God's radical, extraordinary love will continue to honor us and permit us to complete in the much-maligned purgatory. What a blessing it is! Even there my Father's house has many mansions. We must be pure to enter heaven, or we will contaminate all over again. Therefore, he lets our purification continue in a place he created for the purpose. How many of us would be lost if there were no purgatory. Ever thought of that?

It may not be fun, but it beats the alternative. Nobody would choose to live in hell, in total anarchy, dog eat dog, demon consume human, yum, yum, yum. Ugh! That foul place exists, brothers and sisters, and it is beyond our imagining what it really is. There is no respite, no way out, not ever, and you are Satan's plaything for all eternity, a plaything for every ugly creature down there. Dear God! No, no, my brothers and sisters, make very sure that you have given your life to Jesus. Do not take your salvation for granted. Do not be complacent, I beg you.

Some have told me that they can inherit heaven because they were "born Catholic." There's no such person. Sorry. You're born naked like everyone else. This is every man for himself. It's your faith God needs to test, not your Granny's! And don't hang back because your significant others aren't interested. That's between them and their God. He has his ways of bringing his people. Just trust him and start by putting your own life under his loving protection. Had I not done that, Satan would have had my guts for garters, swallowed me alive, and I'd be gone forever. I'm the white sheep of my family! Too bad, so sad! I can pray for them now, though, and that's power. Don't be complacent because you know God loves you, or even that he did miracles for you. He showed up on my life in London, too, didn't he? It didn't save my sorry soul, did it? His love demanded my personal agreement. I had to be willing to learn to live his ways, in word and deed, according to his will for my life. He needed that 'yes', the famous yes of Mary, the yes that changed the world. When he got that from me, we were cracking. Then, he meant business, but only after I did! It's a reciprocal relationship, a two way street. If you will, he will. Period. That's his radical love. He will never impose.

Jesus came, and he's soon to return. Now, it's our move, one by one. The ever-deepening darkness of Satan in the world and in the Church, as we have seen, is making the things of this world look brighter and brighter. This makes it harder and harder for people to see God at all, never mind in spirit and truth as love, light, joy and laughter. The whispering hiss of invisible darkness is killing, stealing and destroying the desire for goodness and pure enjoyment of life. God is presented as a killjoy, brothers and sisters, just waiting to pounce on us for having fun. Ridiculous! He invented laughter, conversation, music and dance, for goodness' sake. Why do we think that ordinary holiness is supposed to be dry and mealy mouthed? Why do we think we have to walk across the floor on tiptoe? Is sound forbidden in the heaven that rings with God's praises and angels screaming Holy, Holy, Holy at every heartbeat? God love us, indeed, if we can't make noise! Here it is, beloved. Prepare yourself. Humans make noise! All kinds of noise! And who made us? God tells us to shout in the assembly, heaven forbid. He tells us to clap our hands. Oh, no! Yes, he does! He wants to hear from us so he knows we're still alive down here! He "inhabits the praises of his people," and they'd better be loud.

I've been asked, "Where did you pick up these strange notions?"

Why, in the Catholic Church! It's the only one I know and it's the only one I've ever known. The only God I've ever known I met there, too. Don't blame me. Blame him! He's done a great job of turning this miserable, depressed, wild, independent, 'free spirit' at death's door, into a joyfully free sheep, happy to let the Shepherd do the thinking and mine only to obey, no longer with blind faith, but with enlightened faith. To him be the glory. My life is a great life; I can't stress it enough. I now let God do the worrying, and I do the praying and praising. That makes us a great team: for him to talk, me to listen, and both to converse. I believed, obeyed and had the sense, or desperation, to seek Jesus through his Mother, Mary! What a woman! Any woman's touch goes a long way, but hers? She is as high as heaven and has its whole ear to assist her to shine her grace on us. She's human, has suffered, has loved, has served, has obeyed and kept every law that any human could keep, and kept her Son to it, too! No broken law, no sin! She knows the way. Plus, she is very strong, accelerates things and keeps us grounded. Time without number, she held me down when I was on the run! We must become as fully human as she! What does that mean? Many things, but certainly it means you have full permission to stop pretending to be a person and embrace the freedom to become the one that you are. Look at you, get to enjoy you, throw away the things about you that you don't like, add the things you do like and do it all with Jesus and for Jesus. You'll fall in love with the pair of you before you know it! Love is freedom! Radical love is radical freedom! Wheeeee!

You have seen how I started out, ticked with my lot in Christ, a most reluctant bride. I was angry to be called. I loved the world and the life I lived. I had my heart set on marrying the love of my life. Then Jesus called. I was more "religious" than the religious. Some thought I was crazy. Who's to say? But I had my eye fixed on that Promised Land! They laughed; they scorned, too bad. I went searching, in and out of the Church, to find that Promised Land, and, finally, I get it. I'm at peace. I knew it from the beginning. I just had to go all the way back to find it. The Catholic Church is the true church.

Christ birthed this Church from his heart. Therefore, whatever we've done with it, right or wrong, so be it. It's past the point of arguing. It's what we have; it's who we are, and it's here to stay. Our sacred, mysterious and, on occasion, spectacular worship will always be ours. The honor of sitting down with Jesus and opening our hearts to his living presence at Adoration will always be ours. If that's all there is, it's everything! But it's not. There's so much more. Jesus has been true to his Church. Now he wants more than a church; he wants a Kingdom. Moreover, that's our job. He will have it, and soon. For there is no better place to build it than where he started, with his Church.

I have come to love it, warts and all; for I know that this Bride will rise up, holy, without spot or wrinkle, crying out, "Come, Lord Jesus, come. The Spirit and the Bride say, 'Come, Maranatha!'"

And he will come!

THE END

Printed in the United States
134923LV00003B/208/P

9 781432 732677